THE NEXT RED WAVE

THE NEXT RED WAVE

HOW CONSERVATIVES CAN BEAT LEFTIST AGGRESSION, RINO BETRAYAL & DEEP STATE SUBVERSION

JORDAN SEKULOW

WITH BENJAMIN SISNEY AND MATTHEW CLARK

CENTER STREET

New York Nashville

Center Street
Hachette Book Group
1290 Avenue of the Americas, New York, NY 10104
centerstreet.com
twitter.com/centerstreet

First edition: September 2019

Center Street is a division of Hachette Book Group, Inc. The Center Street name and logo are trademarks of Hachette Book Group, Inc.

The publisher is not responsible for websites (or their content) that are not owned by the publisher.

Library of Congress Control Number: 2019944337

ISBNs: 978-1-5460-8250-7 (hardcover), 978-1-5460-8251-4 (ebook)

Printed in the United States of America

LSC-C

10 9 8 7 6 5 4 3 2 1

For Anna, my wife
&
Sophie, my daughter

CONTENTS

Foreword by Dr. Jay Sekulow.. ix

1. Preparing for the Next Red Wave—Winds are Forming 1

2. Elections Have Consequences 9

3. We Could Lose.. 19

4. The Deep State Rises.. 35

5. Crashing the Tea Party... 49

6. The Deep State Swamp Festers as the Virus of
   Deception Spreads 69

7. Exposing the Den of Vipers—The ACLJ FOIA Practice.... 92

8. Your Voice—Global Impact...110

CONTENTS

9. Defeating Genocide 122

10. Fighting for Life and Winning: Defeating the
    Abortion Distortion 154

11. Fake News 178

12. The Sacred Duty to Vote 196

13. Redress of Grievances 216

    Acknowledgments 229

    Notes 231

    Index 253

    About the Authors 267

FOREWORD

By Dr. Jay Sekulow

MY CAREER in constitutional law began quite unexpectedly in 1987 when, as a thirty-one-year-old attorney, I was offered the chance to argue a religious speech case that had made its way to the Supreme Court of the United States. I won that case 9–0[1] and quickly realized there was a legal void that needed to be filled in this country. So, in the most grassroots way possible—my wife, Pam, writing the newsletters, my sons, Jordan and Logan, helping fold and mail them from our kitchen table (which we keep in one of our offices today)—we founded a legal organization to fight for constitutionally guaranteed religious liberty. That organization is the American Center for Law and Justice (ACLJ).

Now, even with offices around the country and international affiliates strategically placed around the world, I never forget how it all started—on a table at home with the whole family being involved. I know that this beginning impacted Jordan's interest in politics, law, and grassroots organizing at a young age. At the time, I did not know where it would take him or that one day he would be writing a book about how to utilize the tactics he has learned to keep our conservative ideas and principles on paths to victory.

While I began my constitutional law career as a trial by fire, I did not go from one Supreme Court case to another. In fact, much of the work done between the dozen oral arguments I have presented at our nation's highest Court was carried out at a very local level. I cannot count how many city councils, county commissions, and even school boards I appeared before while advocating for our clients. Jordan attended a lot of those meetings and saw how local government decisions could ultimately end up before the Supreme Court. In a sense, these experiences tie directly into what this book is all about. Of course, presidential and statewide federal elections are important. Yet our local political institutions—like school boards, city councils, county commissions, and state legislatures—have a tremendous impact to this day on my work and that of my many colleagues at the ACLJ. We continue to have ACLJ attorneys appear before city councils and county commissions to protect First Amendment rights even as we have attorneys preparing cases to be heard by the Supreme Court and international tribunals.

Everyone has an opportunity to go a step further than voting in elections. By reading this book, you will learn the value of becoming involved in your local and state governments; you will likely be surprised how easy it can be to get elected at a local level or join the leadership of a county political party. By getting involved, you will make an impact that often can be felt all the way to Washington—in Congress, federal courts, and even the White House.

Pundits often say that a key to a political party's electoral success lies in fielding great candidates. Never forget that a great field of candidates includes candidates for the U.S. Senate, the U.S. House, state offices, and *local* government offices. In fact, great local government candidates can have a direct, positive impact on their communities. Do a good job locally and your constituents will likely look to you for guidance on whom to vote for in top-of-the-ballot races. Thus, you truly have the opportunity to affect your city, county, and state, as well as the nation. We preach this regularly on our radio broadcast, and I just cannot underscore it enough: take the next step in civic and political involvement and the issues you care about will get attention and, ultimately, your ideas may be adopted into good laws. That's where it starts.

We also must not ignore the continued attempts to silence conservative speech. I spearheaded the ACLJ's efforts in defending and ultimately defeating the Internal Revenue Service (IRS) in its much publicized attempts to stifle conservative speech by small grassroots organizations—Tea Party groups, pro-life organizations, and various conservative organizations it perceived to be a threat to its liberal worldview. Our brave clients stood up to the IRS and won. Maybe you are beginning to notice a theme: individuals willing to go that extra step to fight against feared government institutions, and willing to take the risks that come with the fight. To file a legal action, a lawyer must have a client. At the ACLJ, our clients decide to take that next step as part of their civic duty. We just stand with them in the fight.

Today, we continue to battle the Deep State. I am pretty confident this is no longer seen as some sort of conspiracy by reasonable people willing to look past partisan politics. As Jordan's book thoroughly documents, federal bureaucrats are engaged in a very real, ongoing effort to undermine duly elected leaders because they disagree with their policies. We at the ACLJ are continuing to fight back in court;[2] and, as the book will show you, we have exposed numerous attempts by Deep State actors, even in some of our nation's top law enforcement positions, to undermine our commander in chief. From the outset, Jordan and his coauthors have been directly involved in the ACLJ's Government Accountability Project and Freedom of Information Act (FOIA) practice.

We will never stop fighting, but we need more of you—like-minded citizens—to take *your* next step in civic and political engagement. Voting is very important, but there is so much more that can be done.

Jordan and his coauthors have unique backgrounds in law and politics. While all three are attorneys, they have each spent time in the world of partisan politics—at the point where politics intersects with the law. I never imagined my son working for three presidential campaigns, dragging me out to the Iowa Caucuses along the way, all while continuing to advance in bare-knuckle politics. Grassroots is in his blood, and that makes sense, but I have been proud to see him rise through the ranks of local and statewide races to reach the top tier of politics—senior presidential campaign staff.

Jordan even figured out a way to stay involved in presidential politics during his first semester in law school, when he consulted on a presidential campaign and used his semester breaks and weekends to hit the campaign trail. After one more presidential campaign under his belt, where he rose to the level of senior adviser, he rejoined the ACLJ full-time and now cohosts our daily, live radio show, *Jay Sekulow Live*, with me. Often, Jordan hosts the show while I am away for a trial or other legal matter, and he brings his unique knowledge about campaigns and politics to enrich the show for our audience.

Jordan was joined in the endeavor to write this book by two excellent coauthors. Benjamin Sisney serves as senior counsel for litigation and public policy at the ACLJ's Washington, D.C., office, following five years in private practice, a judicial clerkship for a United States district judge, and a legal fellowship for a U.S. senator on Capitol Hill. Matthew Clark serves as senior counsel for digital advocacy at the ACLJ. Previously, he served as a judicial law clerk for the chief judge of the Court of Appeals of Virginia. He has worked on multiple statewide political campaigns, including two election recounts. He has authored pieces for the *Washington Post, Washington Times,* and *Washington Examiner* while also serving as a contributing editor to Red-State.com. At Regent University, he cofounded and served as editor in chief of the *Regent Journal of Law and Public Policy,* a legal publication he cofounded with Jordan. Jordan, Matt, and Ben are all graduates of Regent University School of Law.

The message of this book is critical. Elections have consequences. The president nominates and the U.S. Senate confirms Supreme Court justices. A successful conservative presidential campaign is great...but not if that new president is stonewalled by Congress every step of the way legislatively—via nominations, and even by pointless, distracting investigations that lead nowhere.

I am proud of my son's accomplishments and believe this book is so important, now more than ever, in providing a guide to future conservative victories. There will always be electoral setbacks, but many of those can be corrected in two to four years. That's the beauty of the American governmental structure that our founders so wisely built for us. But our political opponents evolve with the times. The time to prepare for a new form of political battle is now.

Young or old, you will learn a lot from this book and come away feeling encouraged about the power you have to put our conservative ideas into action.

You are about to learn how to get involved, how to win, how to combat the Deep State, how to expose and avoid fake news, and how to defeat the radical Left's agenda. Start reading. There's no time to waste.

THE NEXT RED WAVE

CHAPTER 1

PREPARING FOR THE NEXT RED WAVE—WINDS ARE FORMING

THE NEXT RED WAVE is coming: November 3, 2020.

The Deep State bureaucracy—while certainly weakened over the last few years by investigations, firings, and scandals—will stop at nothing to undermine the conservative agenda, even when that's the agenda chosen by the American voter. The liberal bureaucracy will continue to work alongside former liberal government officials from, yes, the Obama-Biden administration and Team Clinton. In the upcoming election, the Left's most prized goal is not to win control of the U.S. Senate, maintain control of the U.S. House of Representatives, obtain a majority of the governors' mansions, or win a tremendous number of state and local races. For liberal activists, those objectives are completely secondary, if they are on their minds at all. Goal Number 1— exclusively—will be defeating President Donald J. Trump, by whatever means necessary.

A red wave that surpasses the turnout figures of the historic 2016 election will be the only way for conservatives to win back the House, keep control of the Senate, and most important, keep President Trump in the White House.

Our opponents won't be caught off guard by President Trump

again. I promise you, the Democratic National Committee (DNC) and liberal, activist organizations began working on plans to defeat President Trump in 2020 before he was even inaugurated in 2017. In fact, we[1] have evidence of FBI officials attempting to undermine President Trump as he was preparing to take the oath of office back in 2016 and continuing those activities after he became commander in chief.

The radical Left relentlessly forces its liberal agenda on the American people. Even when Republican majorities controlled both houses of Congress, the deck felt stacked against us. The confirmation hearings for Supreme Court Justice Brett Kavanaugh, while ultimately successful on the thinnest of margins, were a good reminder of the chaos liberals can cause, even when they are in the minority. Since Justice Kavanaugh's confirmation, liberals have taken the House of Representatives. While that will not affect nominations requiring Senate confirmation, like cabinet positions and judicial nominees, it will—in the short term—affect conservative legislative priorities. We need to deliver to our President a solid, conservative House and keep building on our successes in the Senate.

Sure, even when the Republicans controlled the House and the Senate, we were frustrated. We were so close to repealing *all* of Obamacare and defunding Planned Parenthood, yet the Republican majorities failed us. In fact, we almost lost the Kavanaugh confirmation because of a weak, RINO (Republican In Name Only) Senate majority. This is why we are not just blindly calling for the election of *Republican* majorities; we're calling for the election of *conservative* majorities in both houses of Congress.

We deserve better. All Americans deserve better. We deserve the legislative priorities we voted for in 2016, and we have a president willing to sign those priorities into law. We face a real uphill battle against fired-up Democrats, from the moderates to the far Left, and at least two years of a divided Congress.

The so-called progressives too often succeed in forcing their leftist agenda on the American people, while the Republican majority we elected relies, with some exceptions, on President Trump to accomplish their goals. It is one reason why the House was lost to the Democrats in 2018.

President Trump has done a great job, but he needs a Congress that is willing to fully implement the policies he was elected to enact. Republicans in Congress, especially Republican majorities, cannot be wasted, as they were in the immediate aftermath of President Trump's victory. We saw a Republican majority House and Senate unable to deliver on key conservative goals. One example is the repeal of Obamacare.

While we are thankful that many so-called moderate Republicans have chosen to retire, it will take a red wave in 2020 to get the legislative agenda back on track so that the burden does not fall completely on President Trump.

He is working tirelessly for the American people, willing to cut bipartisan deals, but the Left wants none of it. The Left's goal is to defeat President Trump, who is arguably the most effective Republican president in decades. He is effective because he doesn't play by the old rules, which conservatives have opposed for many years. He is draining the swamp, and it is our job to fight alongside him against the Left, the elitist (and, dare we say, fake news) mainstream media, the Democrats, and the Deep State bureaucracy.

We deserve politicians who keep their promises. Aren't their promises the reason we took the trouble to go to the polls to vote for them? The only way to force action and hold our elected officials accountable is to know the issues and engage the political process. But doing that requires more than just fulfilling our civic duty at the ballot box. It requires being actively engaged in public discourse between elections. Battles—important battles—are won far more often in the court of public opinion than in any federal courtroom. These battles affect our lives every day.

If we allow broken political promises, political apathy, and the virus of bureaucratic deception to continue to erode the conservative agenda we chose, we could quickly lose the strong America we have been building since the 2016 election. Remember, we have already lost the House. Everything is on the table in 2020.

It's time to fight back and come together to generate the next red wave. We can't wait another moment. Now is the time to do it. It really is up to us. The clock is ticking. With President Trump's energy and willingness to relentlessly campaign and fight for the ideas we believe in, the wind is forming to create the next red wave.

Yet we must not forget that the Deep State bureaucracy will stop at nothing to undermine the conservative agenda—even when that's the agenda chosen by you, the American voter. You didn't elect the bureaucracy, but does it matter? The radical Left continues to ferociously force its liberal agenda on the American people. The radical Left is relentless. Why aren't we? The liberal, elitist mainstream media is muddling the truth with fake news and leftist propaganda. Whom can you trust? The Republican majority in both houses of Congress that *was* elected has, so far, proven itself incompetent—both feckless in its convictions and ineffective in accomplishing even the slightest reforms. Because of that, Republicans lost the House to leftist Democrats bent on destroying everything we have been building.

The deck seems stacked against us. It is. We deserve better.

America will never be perfect. But it can be better. A lot better. **Yet if the America of tomorrow is better than the America of today, that is a victory.** How much better depends on you.

There are things you can do, actions you can take to make America better. But it doesn't start in Washington. Yes, we hope the current administration, along with a stronger conservative majority in the Senate, can radically reform, repeal, and replace outdated, liberal policies and the out-of-control bureaucracy. But we're realists. Washington never really fixes anything. It starts right where you are. Without control of the House, that statement has never been truer for conservatives.

Think about it. Our political system allows us to choose our decision makers. But it does not allow us to control the decisions they make. We elect them, but they, not us, are the ones who actually make the decisions that shape our communities, our states, and our nation.

Those decisions come in the form of committee votes, council resolutions, budgets, legislation, amendments to legislation, directives, executive orders, and special appointments. Even when we vote yes or no on state questions and ballot referenda, we might think that we decided them. But guess who voted to include (or not to include) that question on the ballot? And guess who drafted the language of the question in order to make it more or less appealing? That was done by the decision makers we elected.

Some of these decisions make headlines. Many of them, however, do not. They just happen. Quietly. In a city council session you never heard about. So while we are right to focus on the presidential, House, and Senate races in 2020, we must never forget the importance of local races—right down to city council and school board.

After all, we are working forty, sixty, maybe even eighty hours a week, raising a family, and paying bills. Some of us are taking evening classes at the local university or community college to better our lives. Others are taking care of an elderly parent or perhaps a family member who needs some extra care. Some of us have our own medical challenges. We try to stay active in our churches and places of worship. And wow, our kids' sports teams sure have a lot of practices. We vote every November, or at least most Novembers.

By the time Saturday arrives, the last thing in the world we want to do is call our representative and leave a voicemail message to express why we want him or her to vote a certain way on an amendment to somebody's bill that's going to be heard by some committee next week.

But then, when the next week rolls around, we skim a headline in the paper or on our phone announcing that committee's vote that amended a bill to spend state money (which means *our* money) on abortions. And we think to ourselves, "That's horrible. That's not what I wanted my representative to do. How in the world did that happen?"

Even worse, the news media may not want you to know that your state or local government decided to spend your hard-earned tax dollars promoting abortion, so the headline might use terms like "reproductive health" or "family planning" in describing the latest measure passed.

But even when we have an idea of what's going on behind the scenes, by the time we get off work on a typical night, the last thing we want to do is drive over to the city council building to attend a hearing or go to a precinct meeting to vote on our county's party leadership or platform. Then, months later, we hear the news that our party voted somebody into leadership who is well known for being hostile to homeschooling or religious schools. And we mention to our spouse, "Can you believe what's happening to our party?"

We are tired. And understandably so. There's only so much gas in the tank. It's just too much. But we have time to recharge right now. Time to recruit great candidates up and down the ballot. The 2018 elections should be a wakeup call. While conservatives fared well in many statewide races, they fared poorly in the House, where Democrats seized the majority. This is a House Democrat majority bent on investigating every action by the executive branch; their leadership has no interest in legislating and some of their far-left members are calling for the President of the United States to be impeached because they don't like his policies.

Regardless, we do more than choose our decision makers. Choosing them, by voting, is a critical first step. But it's just the *first step*. We have the right, the privilege, and the moral obligation not just to choose them, but also to influence them once they are in office.

Decision makers are listening to somebody when they make the decisions. It sure better be us.

You can be certain others are clamoring for their attention, and exerting pressure in obvious and subtle ways. Special interests. Lobbyists. They're all fighting for a seat at the table. Shouldn't we?

So let us not overlook something here that is critically important: we *get* to choose our decision makers. Stop and think about that for a moment. Don't take that for granted. Do you realize how incredible that is? Citizens of this country are recipients of such a special gift. So many people living elsewhere in the world could hardly comprehend not only our freedoms, but our ability to choose our leaders. But we have to actually choose them. That means we have to vote.

It's not just a right. It's not just a civic exercise. **Our vote is actually a sacred duty.** Because it's a God-given right, it is a responsibility, even a biblical calling. If God has blessed us to live in a land where "we the people" are the government, and God has established and ordained the government, then it becomes our spiritual responsibility to vote. "Vote your conscience" isn't just a catchphrase. It's a biblical imperative.

The next red wave won't happen overnight. It won't happen in one race. It won't happen in one state. It won't happen by casting just one vote. It will require each and every one of us to engage— to really engage. That means doing more than just going to the polls on Election Day and pulling the lever for one of the names in front of you. The next red wave is about far more than just voting. That's why we wrote this book. It's not for politicians— though they could certainly learn from it. It's for you. It's for we the people. You can make the difference. You can *be* the difference. You can see we are up against a lot, but we can win. Again.

CHAPTER 2

ELECTIONS HAVE CONSEQUENCES

ELECTIONS HAVE CONSEQUENCES. *Every* election matters. We can't overstate the importance of that truth. If you need another reminder, remember 2018 and look to the current Democrat Speaker of the House.

Those consequences extend beyond the federal level.

Our county commissioners dictate tax breaks, benefits, and services for groups whose philosophy and mission we strongly agree with or strongly disagree with.

For example, many county commissions exert authority over zoning decisions. Sometimes this authority is exercised by zoning boards or some municipal (city or town) form of government. These zoning authorities often grant permission to groups that we don't want in our communities allowing them to do business in them anyway. Yet, ironically, the same boards may deny permission to entities whose presence and influence we *do* want, such as churches, Bible-study groups, and faith-based ministries.

Sometimes, a zoning authority's decisions are based on partisan political animus or even fear of retribution from the PC police, favoring the latest politically correct religion—let's say

Islam—over a disfavored religion—let's say Christianity. The zoning board could vote to provide county services—such as extending water and sewer lines—to an Islamic community center in a rural community, while refusing to do the same for numerous area churches.[1]

In other cases, it's not necessarily animosity per se toward religion that drives these hostile zoning decisions. **Many times, it's just the bottom line. Money.**

Religious organizations enjoy certain tax exemptions, and they do not typically generate a taxable product or service. As a result, their presence within a town, city, county, or district simply does not generate the same amount of revenue that a commercial enterprise would generate operating in that same space. The result, however, is the same. **Disfavor toward religion**—in this case manifested by greed.

Religion-based organizations often face uphill battles when they try to find places to fulfill their calling and serve their communities. They often face challenges when they need to move and when it is time to expand into a bigger structure.[2] Do we want our local governments to make it difficult for these groups to carry out their missions? Did we even know it was happening? Have we directly asked our state and local governments to explain their positions to us on these issues?

On a different front, our city, county, and state governments siphon our wallets dry in unfathomable ways. But we must begin to fathom their reach. We must begin to realize just how influential local and state governments are when it comes to our communities. Yes, in 2020 it is critical to reelect President Trump, maintain a conservative Senate majority, and retake the U.S. House. But we cannot forget what's going on right at home in our communities. If we are going to get involved, let's get completely engaged—educate ourselves on the issues, participate in grassroots activism, and ultimately, persuade our friends, neighbors, and colleagues to get out and vote.

Here is an example: Our state and local governments enact policies that either attract business, enterprise, and investments or discourage them. Tax breaks, which tend to encourage and promote business, play a big part in that dance. But special interests can abuse tax breaks by lobbying legislatures in order to use them to give those special interests an advantage over their competitors. They do this by making it so that only those entities that satisfy x, y, and z requirements qualify for the tax break. And guess what, only the businesses wealthy enough and sophisticated enough to meet the requirements for those tax breaks (or that can afford the army of lawyers it takes to understand the tax code) can possibly qualify. But this does not make tax breaks bad. This makes the rules for how businesses, or people, can qualify for tax breaks very important. Lobbyists are influencing these state and local decision makers. Are we?

We can't say it enough—focus on the big races of 2020—the White House and Congress—but make sure you're also voting wisely for all those other state and local elected offices, as well as those often confusing ballot proposals or propositions.

Having President Trump on the ballot will drive voter turnout that breaks all records—if Democrats can find a serious opponent. If so, Republicans down the ballot can ride a true Trump wave. But make sure you choose the right Republicans in the primary to appear on the ballot with President Trump. Democrats did a pretty darn good job recruiting House candidates in 2018. Republicans must do better in 2020.

BACK TO BUSINESS

Our small businesses need tax breaks. So do our large businesses. If your business pays less in taxes, you have more money to pay your bills and your employees' salaries and to increase your profits at the end of the day. If your business is paying more in taxes, then the opposite happens. It is not rocket science. And these fundamental, basic economic principles hold true whether your business is big or small.

Businesses that have higher profits hire more people. They build new buildings and hire contractors and labor. They sell more products and/or services that are taxed, and they encourage more people to move to or spend money within that jurisdiction—which means the state and local governments actually make more money in the end! That's why the tax law that went into effect in 2018 is so important, and it's why we've seen record economic growth and jobs numbers as a result.

Taxes matter. And not just in Washington. Sales tax, property tax, car and boat tax, meals tax, license fees, and the list goes on and on. The government has figured out how to take your hard-earned money in many ways. Now, of course, not all taxes are bad. Roads, law enforcement, emergency services, schools, libraries...these things cost money. If we want our state and local governments to provide these things, then we have to fund them.

CANDIDATES MATTER

But this highlights the point here: So many of these decisions about how to spend our tax money are made in our state and local governments. We elect them. In many cases, we *know* them.

We can tell them what we want. We can tell them what we do not want. Somebody is. Why are we not at the table? In 2020, with President Trump at the top of the ticket, we can make sure we influence those local and state officials who will run as Trump Republicans. Let's make sure that, once they are in office, they govern like Trump Republicans.

It's interesting, too, how, during election season, every candidate is for tax cuts. But do we know who will follow through on that commitment? We know that President Trump is doing so at the federal level. But not all candidates are trustworthy on that point. Be skeptical. Are you being fed talking points when you see an ad on television or when you call the candidate's campaign office? Or are you hearing from someone who has developed a meaningful grasp of economic principles and realities that perhaps only someone who has run their own business could have developed?

There are members of our communities who have had to face difficult decisions and now have the experience to lead. They have been forced to lay off employees, or cut them back to part-time, or not hire new ones—all because their state and/or local governments thought they knew better than the people what was best for them and mandated an artificial minimum wage.[3] They have faced an out-of-control regulatory behemoth government. They know firsthand how destructive government can be. Maybe they were forced to provide healthcare benefits and, as a result, had to lay off employees. What once was a perk has now become a right. That is the travesty of Obamacare. Citizen legislators—regular Americans who have had real-life experiences with bad government— can often make the best elected representatives. It's how our nation was built, and it may just be time to get back to that.

Again—and we can't stress this enough—candidate recruitment is the key in down-ballot races.

Yet the politicians we get often prove to be fickle. They run as true, sincere conservatives. They claim to be stalwart, constitutional conservatives (a term overused these days by candidates who do not appear to even understand its meaning). But then, lo and behold, after the election, the principled conservative promised to us in his or her campaign mailers is nowhere to be found.

He said he was a conservative. She said she had always stood for limited government, for families, and for tax breaks. Trust us, they said. If you really want a conservative, then donate to our campaigns. So we did. And now we wonder what happened.

Instead, we find our representative, delegate, or state senator is suddenly (or, sometimes, not so suddenly) a "moderate" who is all about such noble concepts as working with the other side and bipartisanship (which often just means our representative voted for the other side's bill without getting anything in return). And again, you wonder what happened.

Bipartisanship should be used cautiously or in times of emergency. Outside of that, in today's political environment, **when Republican politicians say "bipartisan," we hear "coward."**

Given what happened in the 2018 midterm elections, we can see only three issues that are even remotely feasible to solve through truly bipartisan efforts before the 2020 elections. They are:

1. Funding and building the southern border wall combined with a pathway to permanent residency or citizenship for the millions of undocumented, illegal immigrants here—that would include tremendous vetting (no criminals) and a long path to legal residency or citizenship (including payment of back taxes on earnings, as an example). We also understand the compromise would have to include Deferred Action for

Childhood Arrivals (DACA)[4] with restrictions on when the minors entered and if they have otherwise been law-abiding, but for the fact that they were brought to the United States as minors illegally but, truly, at no fault of their own.

2. Reforming healthcare by defunding Obamacare and creating a better alternative for Americans. (But even this is tenuous, as the Left has made clear that it is pushing for single-payer healthcare or no changes, something over which conservatives certainly must not compromise.)

3. Infrastructure. We all notice our crumbling infrastructure. This is an issue that can unite Republicans and Democrats if, and only if, Democrats in the House have any interest in passing legislation that may be seen as a victory by President Trump. In reality, better infrastructure would be a victory for all Americans, regardless of their political persuasion or lack thereof, just as long as it doesn't become a big-spending boondoggle that winds up building more bridges to nowhere.

Each of these will require the Democrats to compromise with Republicans. All too often, it is only the other way around. It will require political fortitude from conservatives.

Are we conservatives too shy to publicly engage in real politics? The Left surely isn't.

It's natural to be a little shy when it comes to politics. It makes perfect sense. But that does not change a critical reality: the people running for these offices still make many of the decisions that affect us, our families, our businesses, our schools, and even our churches.

ELECTIONS SET POLICY PRIORITIES

For example, consider abortion. Some significant laws, rules, and policies concerning abortion happen at the national level. We'll get to them later and walk through some significant victories we have realized since the 2016 presidential election. But we must also fully understand how much abortion policy is dictated right in our own states—by lawmakers and executives over whom we have a much greater degree of influence than we do over our national leaders.

In fact, several years ago, the city council in New York City (and then in Baltimore) passed an ordinance essentially requiring pro-life pregnancy centers to promote abortion. As their name implies, these pro-life centers' entire existence is predicated on defending life. They care for women in need and provide advice, care, support, and even adoption assistance for women and their unborn babies. It's all they do. It's why they exist. Under the radar and under the guise of transparency, New York City required these pro-life institutions to spread pro-abortion propaganda.

What started in one city spread to another and then another and then another. Then, states like California and Hawaii passed similar laws, each slightly worse than the last.

At the American Center for Law and Justice (ACLJ)—the constitutional law firm where we all work—we fought back in court. After years of litigation against this unconstitutional government coercion and violation of these pro-life centers' free speech rights, we won at the U.S. Supreme Court—striking down the California law and allowing us to use that decision to defeat similar laws in other states.

This example shows how laws can spread across the country. Sometimes they are good, like those requiring child-safety seats.

Just a few decades ago, such seats weren't required anywhere. Today, they are required everywhere in this country, and save countless lives.

The example also shows the importance of fighting back against bad laws, to prevent them from spreading like an unconstitutional virus.

In our constitutional system of government, we have federalism. This gives a great (but, sadly, shrinking) amount of sovereignty and autonomy to state and local governments. Police power is what it used to be referred to (and still is in the legal system). Welfare, morality, those kinds of things. And in our beautiful, revolutionary system of government, it was understood that **the best government is the government that governs closest to the people**.

It's said that state and local governments are the laboratories of democracy. They get to experiment with laws. And they get to apply them to the particular situations faced in that community. They are not one-size-fits-all.

In other words, the best, most efficient, and most accountable government is local government. Local government matters. But, sadly, it is local government that most of us take for granted and know the least about. This must change if we are to have a shot at restoring our precious United States of America.

National government matters, too, there is no doubt, but **local and state governments just might be where the real key is hidden**. National government and politics often set the tone and broad policies; state and local governments implement them at the most personal level.

The political reality is that there is plenty of overlap—your local elected officials often end up being your governor, representatives, senators, and even president. That's how politics works. Remember, President Trump is the only person in our nation's history who was elected president without having served in any type of government office. Chances are your local school board member will end up being your next representative in Congress. If that's a scary thought, recruit someone to run who shares your values or—it may sound like a crazy notion—start your own campaign.

Nationally, the House and Senate in Washington can completely stonewall the President's conservative agenda. The agenda we thought we voted for. The agenda for which we donated our hard-earned dollars in the form of campaign contributions, volunteered time at phone banks, attended rallies and neighborhood walks, all with the goal of getting out the vote for the conservative agenda we believed these politicians represented. Good candidates, trustworthy candidates, who will support President Trump's conservative agenda are the key to success.

But to have that success, to bring about the next red wave, we must first understand what went wrong.

CHAPTER 3

WE COULD LOSE

IN 2016, WE THOUGHT we had scored the ultimate victory—the White House, the House, and the Senate. So what went wrong?

We thought we voted for Obamacare to be repealed. We thought we voted for Planned Parenthood to be defunded. We thought we voted to drain the swamp. Yet none of that has happened. Why not?

Did we call our senators and representatives—after they were elected? Did we let them know that we still expected them to follow through on the promises they had made to us to earn our financial contributions to their campaigns, and our votes, once they got to Washington? Did we let them know that we would be more than willing to take our campaign contributions and our votes elsewhere if they didn't follow through on their promises? Did we really even know for *whom* we were voting? Do they really know us? Do they even care? Do we?

THE POLITICIANS YOU DESERVE

We deserve politicians who keep their promises. No, seriously, we really do.

Aren't their promises the reason we took the trouble to go to the polls on the way to work, or on the way home after a long day at work, to vote for them? Aren't their promises the reason we contributed to or volunteered for their campaigns?

These campaign promises represent our only way of knowing what they will do once elected. **Now, however, the campaign promise is a euphemism for a lie, the subject of jokes. This is sad.**

Remember some of the classics? Here is one that still stings: "Put the Republicans in charge. They will repeal Obamacare." Yep, definitely still stings.

This one was worse, because it was told over numerous years. "Give us the House," they said, "and we will stand up to President Obama." We gave them the House, but never quite saw the spine we were promised.

"Give us the Senate," they said, "then we can stand up to President Obama." We gave them the Senate, but amazingly, the spine did not appear, until the very end of President Obama's term. Thankfully, finally, Senate Republican leadership held firm and protected Justice Antonin Scalia's seat on the Supreme Court, blocking President Obama's attempt to ramrod a Supreme Court nominee through in his final months in office.

But, in most instances, holding the House and Senate wasn't enough. "Give us the White House," they said, "because that is the only way we can repeal Obamacare, reform our tax code, and defund Planned Parenthood." We gave them the White House and a president who actually followed through on his campaign promises. But Obamacare, more or less, is still the law of the land. **President Trump can only rein in so much of that colossal failure via executive order.** He is doing a great job, the best he can, but Congress passed it into law, so Congress has to repeal it. President Trump is ready to sign the repeal and replacement of Obamacare, but Congress has been unable to get it to his desk.

Thankfully, the House and Senate (surprisingly) enacted comprehensive tax reform—a monumental victory that can't be denied. But what about the rest of what we were promised?

The Republican majority in the House came to an end before President Trump could repeal Obamacare. Legal challenges are under way, but ultimately Congress must get a repeal bill to the President's desk, which is very unlikely, even as the healthcare system continues to fail, until after the 2020 elections.

Another broken promise was taxpayer funding for Big Abortion. Planned Parenthood, the largest abortion business in America, still takes more than half a billion of our hard-earned tax dollars each year—nearly half of its gargantuan budget sucked from our paychecks. Even after it got caught on video selling the body parts of aborted babies, it still takes our money. This is beyond comprehension and makes us mourn for our nation. Even though President Trump promised to sign a bill defunding Planned Parenthood, Congress failed to get one to his desk when our representatives had the chance. Now we are still paying for it, thanks to broken campaign promises and the leaders who broke them.

But it doesn't have to be this way. You deserve campaign promises that will be kept—not lies and political talking points.

Campaign promises should mean something, and they should be important. But to many, they remain nothing more than a joke. And it is easy to see why.

Many were shocked and the Left looked on in horror as President Trump appointed a principled conservative jurist, Neil Gorsuch, to the U.S. Supreme Court. At literally hundreds of campaign rallies, then-candidate Trump promised cheering crowds that he would appoint a conservative to the nation's highest Court, someone who would uphold the Constitution. He even gave people a list of a couple of dozen individuals he promised to pick from.

The shock came when he actually followed through on that promise. No one had expected he would. Why? Because politicians breaking campaign promises has become a national pastime.

Well it's past time that ends.

President Trump, on the other hand, continues to keep his campaign promises. When he had a second opportunity to appoint someone to the Supreme Court, he nominated Brett Kavanaugh, and stood by the nominee while he was skewered by innuendo and phony witnesses attacking his character when he was a teenager. Thankfully, President Trump was unrelenting in his support for Justice Kavanaugh, the circus around his nomination was exposed as a political witch hunt, and Justice Kavanaugh took his rightful seat on the bench. We're proud of Justice Kavanaugh for persevering even with the tremendous toll it took on his family.

But now, far-left Democrats want to impeach him, too![1] So, we have to be ready to keep fighting for Justice Kavanaugh even now that he has been confirmed.

There is a reason why congressional approval ratings are routinely abysmal, but this also presents a puzzle: **Why do the same lawmakers keep getting elected when Congress as a whole is so unpopular?** Well, there are multiple reasons, no doubt. But we submit that our own personal choices, priorities, and inaction play a very real role.

There's a saying that everyone hates Congress, but they sure do love their own member of Congress.[2] The thought behind this saying is that as long as a person's own representatives bring home the bacon, they'll keep getting reelected. In fact, they don't even need to bring home the bacon as long as they can convince their constituents that they are trying and it's the other members' fault that they are not succeeding. At the same time, though, particular members' constituents dislike all the other representatives doing the exact same things for their constituents in other states. This gives us a glimpse of human nature. But we cannot give in to this.

We must demand integrity from our own members of Congress. By the way, we are not condemning, wholesale, representatives who secure a piece of the pie for their states. Many times, if it wasn't going to one state, it would be going to another. As long as Washington is doling out money, representatives of all fifty states will fight for a seat at the table. That's just the way it works. But the way it works is part of what has to change. We must demand fidelity to values, not just earmarks, and Washington shouldn't be doling out billions of dollars for things the private marketplace is perfectly capable of producing.

Regardless, shouldn't Congress be hearing from us about how that money is spent? They are most certainly hearing from others.

BETWEEN THE BALLOT BOXES

The only way to force action and hold your elected officials accountable is to (1) know the issues and (2) engage the political process. But doing that requires doing more than just fulfilling your civic duty at the ballot box. It requires being actively engaged in public discourse *between elections*. Battles—important battles—are won far more often in the court of public opinion than in any federal courtroom. These battles affect your life every single day.

Learning about the issues doesn't require a degree in constitutional law, history, or economics. To a great extent, it just takes paying attention and becoming informed. Read the writings of our Founders and the people who influenced the American idea and American sacrifice. Listen to the radio. Watch the news. Read reliable newspapers and websites.

To whom do we listen? Where we get our information is as important as the information itself. In a world of fake news, leftist media bias, and progressive propaganda, it's incredibly important to get your news from trusted sources.

That's why I cohost a conservative talk radio show, *Jay Sekulow Live*, each and every day, and it's why we work at the ACLJ—to provide the American people, to provide you, with the news and information you need to make informed decisions about where our country should be headed. We go deep behind the headlines, present the facts, analyze the law, and provide insight on the political talking points that are driving the cable news cycle. These are not the only sources, and we'll discuss this more later, but making wise choices about where you get your information is the foundation of being an informed citizen. And being a well-informed citizen is the key to effective civic involvement.

HOW WE ENGAGE THE POLITICAL PROCESS

Next, we want to talk about how we engage the political process. Engage those around you. Don't "get in their face," the way President Obama so infamously encouraged[3] his followers to do on the campaign trail. But engage them. We don't have to be embarrassed or shy about being conservatives who love our country. We are not extremists. We do not have to apologize for loving our nation and the values that have made it special.

If we really understand what we believe, we can defend our values with confidence. It's the same with our religious beliefs or anything else. We have to know what we believe in order to convince someone else to believe it, too.

The power of truth allows us to be persuasive. We do not have to, nor do we even want to, resort to force or intimidation as advocated by the radical Antifa movement (which, ironically, represents the real fascists). We have the upper hand because we are right. We can trust in that.

But we should not allow ourselves to be bullied by "progressive" propaganda and radical leftist attacks.

We don't have to sit quietly by while our constitutional rights are abused and violated. In our American system of government, we choose our Caesar and we decide whether to return him or her to office. We also have an avenue of relief in the courts. We know we can engage our adversaries in the courtroom, stand up for our rights lawfully, and win. Victory is possible. We know this because we have done it. Multiple times, in fact.[4]

THE BUREAUCRATIC DAM THAT STOPPED THE LAST RED WAVE

Take the Tea Party–targeting cases. The Obama-Biden administration illegally targeted hundreds of grassroots political organizations. Why? Because the organizations were conservative (or sounded conservative, because their names included words like "patriot" or "liberty"). Also, they represented a groundswell of individual activism identified as the Tea Party movement. It was a clear and present danger to the Obama administration's radical leftist agenda.

It was a massive, impending red wave, and the Left had to stop it at any cost.

During the lead-up to President Obama's 2012 reelection, the Tea Party became a massive political force. You see, the Tea Party wasn't really a political party at all, but a grassroots movement composed of everyday Americans who were fed up with the political elites spending our future generations into insurmountable debt. In the 2010 midterms, this groundswell of grassroots conservative activism had already swept away the Democrat majority in Congress like a red tidal wave.

The Left had to fight back, but they were losing every which way. The conservative movement's momentum was building exponentially. Then came the Left's best friend, the bureaucracy, to the rescue. Their weapon of choice? The IRS.

Here's how they did it. In order for a nonprofit organization to use all of its resources to advance its mission, it can apply to the IRS for tax-exempt status. The Obama administration knew this. As the conservative groups' applications began to pour in to the IRS, they mysteriously began being held up. Most of them were not being denied, just delayed—indefinitely. These groups were in something of an IRS purgatory, floating in space, unsure of their tax status, as the critical months leading up to President Obama's reelection slipped by.

Predictably, without donors knowing the tax-exempt status of the organizations they were considering donating to and without the organizations themselves knowing if they were going to be able to survive a potential crippling tax bill, the donations dried up.

No tax-exempt status meant no donations. No donations meant they couldn't advocate against President Obama's policies and his political enablers, the Democrat Party, nor could the organizations advocate contrasting policies. They couldn't oppose the President's policies, and they couldn't offer any viable alternatives. A brilliant strategy. Corrupt, but brilliant.

It not only effectively killed the Tea Party, but it also chilled the free speech of the Silent Majority—conservative Americans, many of whom were for the first time engaging in the political process. The story of the Tea Party is both a cautionary tale of the danger posed by the radical Left's weaponization of the bureaucracy and a road map for how we can bring about the next red wave.

But here is the key: we have to stand up and fight where we can. And that's what we did. Representing several dozen clients, the ACLJ sued the Obama IRS. Other organizations filed lawsuits as well. It took more than four and a half years in federal court. It took bravery by our clients. It took resolve by our team of lawyers on the case. It took our donors' support to keep fighting the IRS.

We didn't quit, and in the end, we won. Ultimately, the IRS admitted its grievous violations and apologized in writing. More important, we obtained a federal court order barring the IRS from ever again targeting conservative groups for their political beliefs. Numerous officials involved in the scandal no longer work for the IRS. Its offices dealing with tax-exempt applications have been radically altered. Through their bravery, these plaintiffs fundamentally reshaped the way the IRS operates. This will affect other groups from now on. We can make a difference.

We'll delve further into the *Linchpins of Liberty* case and bureaucratic IRS corruption later, but we chose to preview it here because it shows, clear as day, that we can win. We can claim our appeal to Caesar, so to speak. We have rights, God-given rights, in this country that we can lawfully enforce. It just takes action, commitment, and courage. It takes fully understanding the consequences if we don't.

WHY THE LEFT IS WINNING

It takes more than voting. We voted a powerhouse message across the country in 2016, and even in the 2018 elections, increasing the Senate majority. Conservatives were winning. Their message was heard loud and clear. We changed the course of our government. We can just sit back now and enjoy the fruits of our recent victories, right? Wrong. We lost the House to Democrats in 2018—in some races because of changing demographics but in many others because of bad candidates, including some who ran away from President Trump.[5]

Our generation has watched the conservative agenda—the agenda we voted for—die a protracted death by a thousand cuts: failure to repeal Obamacare; refusal to tackle entitlement reform; continued funding for the Planned Parenthood abortion machine, even after the sickest of truths about its deadly profit-engine were revealed; budget bickering that leads to continued fiscal irresponsibility; and a national debt that crushes our children's future.

Meanwhile, "progressives" succeed in forcing their leftist agenda on the American people through a dogmatic adherence to incremental victories. Abortion. Education. Regulations. And the slow but steady emergence of the behemoth, regulatory Deep State.

There is only so much that President Trump can do through executive orders to stem this tide. Yet the Republican majority you elected refused to understand or implement a "big picture" approach. Instead, it continually snatched defeat from the jaws of victory, refusing to compromise with even its own members to secure even the smallest advances. Splintered and fractured. Turf wars, factions, and popularity cliques. We're not talking about partisanship between the political parties; we're talking about the

Republican Party's refusal to compromise within the conservative movement. This was no doubt a factor in why Republicans lost the House in 2018.

On the other side of the aisle, though, machine-like uniformity appears to prevail. At least on the surface, they play follow-the-leader better than a playground full of elementary school students. The fact that Democrats found a way through all of their blunders—including Nancy Pelosi telling everyone that the Democrats had won, even before people voted[6]—to take back the House is a reminder that party unity can lead to victory, even in the absence of a clear message.

Democrats did a good job of burning down their own party in 2016, but they were quick to reorganize for 2018 with a focus on the U.S. House and state races. It became quickly apparent in the aftermath of the 2016 election that Hillary Clinton literally owned the Democrat Party's apparatus and had rigged the 2016 Democrat primary. Even now, there is an all-out uncivil war being waged in the Democrat Party between the faction led by Senator Bernie Sanders of Vermont and Senator Elizabeth Warren of Massachusetts on one side and the Clinton machine on the other.

The tell-all book[7] by Donna Brazile, the former acting chairwoman of the DNC, exposed the Clinton corruption entrenched at the DNC and added napalm to the fire. Yet, somehow, the Democrats were able to compartmentalize their internal strife, put it behind them, and focus on winning. After taking back the House in 2018, they then went right back to infighting. But conservatives cannot just sit back and watch the Left burn—we have to fight back to win.

As conservatives, we are uniquely positioned to take back not only the Republican Party, but also our nation, with so many moderates having retired or lost their seats. But can we?

We were promised so much on issues that have literally life-and-death implications. And we, the American people, delivered. Bigly. But what is happening in Washington? *Is Congress delivering for President Trump?* Is Congress delivering for us? No. Those promises have been repeatedly broken.

If past is prologue, then the outlook appears bleak. **But these proclivities for failure on the Right are what this book sets out to remedy.**

The broken promises have led to political burnout. We can feel it. It's understandable. If the 2016 presidential and congressional elections didn't send a message, what will? If there was ever a movement against the status quo, that was it. The movement swept the country like a red tsunami, building momentum as it went. How could any politician miss the signal? How could any pundit confuse the message? How could any television host or reporter misunderstand the level of passion so many Americans rose up and displayed?

Yet daily, we see on our televisions, newspapers, and news sites example after example of politicians and pundits willfully distorting the obvious. It's unrelenting. It's the arrogance of elitism on full display. And, in 2018, we got a dose of reality and saw the consequences of both the failures of the Republicans and the vicious tenacity of all those on the Left.

Are we too going to be that unrelenting? Our message is this: We must be. We have no choice.

Voting is crucial. But it will take more than just voting. We have to engage. If we allow broken political promises, political apathy, and the virus of bureaucratic deception to continue to erode the conservative agenda we chose, we could lose our America.

A NEW HOPE

Lest we give in to political despair, we would do well to remember a few things. The message that the American people sent in electing President Trump has not fallen on deaf ears. Despite congressional shenanigans, President Trump has made some drastic changes within the executive branch:

- Reinstating the Mexico City Policy—reversing the Obama-Biden administration's international abortion funding giveaway. This policy prevents U.S. tax dollars from being used to fund abortions internationally. It was first imposed in 1984 by President Ronald Reagan and continued under each successive Republican administration, but was withdrawn during each subsequent Democrat administration. President Trump took it further than any previous president in a stunning display of reverence for the lives of the unborn. As we will explain, these policy changes are having a massive impact, protecting your tax dollars and saving unborn lives.

- Pursuing other pro-life prerogatives. The administration's Department of Health and Human Services (HHS), usually a predictably partisan, pro-abortion federal agency, implemented a new four-year strategic plan of pursuing policies that recognize that **life begins at conception**. Yes, the same HHS that once used Obamacare to force the abortion-pill mandate down the throats of pro-life Americans has now reversed course and is pursuing policies of protecting life.

- Confirming two conservatives to the U.S. Supreme Court. Justice Gorsuch is now on the nation's highest Court, replacing the late Justice Antonin Scalia. This was a campaign promise kept. And make no mistake, this was a tremendous victory for the American people and the Constitution. In addition, Justice Kavanaugh—a true constitutional conservative—is also on the Supreme Court, replacing retired Justice Anthony Kennedy—the Court's "swing vote." Another promise kept.

- Slashing regulations. Under one of President Trump's executive orders, no new regulation may be implemented without two existing regulations being nullified. Another campaign promise kept. Another victory for the American people.
- Restoring our constitutionally protected religious liberties by undoing Obama-era policies that forced religious ministries to violate their consciences or pay debilitating fines. The Obama-Biden IRS and Department of Justice did everything in their power to choke these conservative religious groups—vulnerable charities like the Little Sisters of the Poor—out of existence. President Trump flipped the script and sent a new message: religious beliefs are sacred and protected by our Constitution. Promise kept. Victory.
- Standing up to ISIS and supporting our military service members. President Trump has protected America from enemies both foreign and domestic—just as he said he would. Soon after taking office in 2017, he sent a message to radical Islamic terrorists when he ordered the nonnuclear Mother of All Bombs (MOAB) dropped on a jihadist stronghold. Since then, our military has dropped more ordnance on ISIS and its radical Islamic ilk in a year than the Obama-Biden administration did in eight years.
- The righteous might and power of the U.S. military has been unleashed. President Trump and his senior military advisers revised the rules of engagement so now our troops can win. He put the generals back in charge and got out of their way. The message he has sent to ISIS and to the world is one we've been longing for an American president to send for years. An-

other promise kept. Victories happening daily. ISIS is nearly defeated on all fronts.

So yes, we've enjoyed real victories. **But every victory won can be taken back from us.** Our adversaries have gone "all in" to get back to the way things were when they called the shots. Does it look like the statists pulling the strings of the Deep State are surrendering? Does the mainstream media appear complacent and content? Or does it feel like a multifaceted political war machine is in full attack mode? Make no mistake, they are fighting for their version of America. They will stop at nothing. Please, please understand this.

But thinking, or even knowing, that we are right is meaningless unless we also take action. We will discuss not only how to equip yourself for political battle, but also how to engage in the fight. We will cover some key ways we can fight back for our cherished, one-of-a-kind nation.

We'll also cover some real and relevant examples of how fighting back can, in fact, lead to victory. In other words, we will show you how we can win, by showing you how we have won.

On a more sobering note, but one equally critical, we will give very real examples of how failing to fight back, or even just failing to stay committed to the end, results in defeat.

We might not win every battle. But if we fight, we will win some. On the other hand, if we refuse to fight, or if we surrender halfway through, we can count on losing every time.

Our complacency, our fear, our apathy are precisely what our opponents are counting on. It's the proverbial battle of attrition. Advocates of big government, out-of-control taxes, mandates, unelected and unaccountable bureaucratic power and pages and pages of regulations, restrictions on religious liberty, and soft but hardening tyranny all display a relentless commitment to waiting us out. They think that, after a few losses, we will become frustrated, bored, and unengaged. Notice, the Left never loses its energy.

We're too busy to march in the streets (maybe it's because we work for a living). Many of us don't like to draw attention to ourselves or our personal beliefs. Just let us live our lives.... But things are changing. The country is changing. American politics are evolving. We are entering uncharted territory.

If we are not in the game to win, we lose. If we are not willing to engage wholeheartedly, we lose.

What will it take to win?

It's time to fight back for America. It's time to fight for the next red wave.

CHAPTER 4

THE DEEP STATE RISES

THE ELATION OF CONSERVATIVES following the 2016 election quickly eroded barely hours into President Trump's term in office as a new, sinister force reared its ugly head. We thought draining the swamp meant sending packing those politicians who no longer cared about their constituents.

But the next red wave will require more than just electing conservatives and throwing leftist elected politicians out of office.

Winning the election wasn't the half of it. Draining the swamp brought out something that can only be described as a swamp creature. It's a force that most of America didn't know existed. We didn't know that there was a deep rot in our government that an election couldn't fix. But there is. It is real.

The Deep State is real. It's functioning at this very moment. Entrenched operatives with a political agenda—and a sincerely held belief that they know what's best for the country and what's best for you—are quietly working to accomplish their mission. What is their mission? What are they trying to accomplish? And why?

First, let's take a look at what the Deep State is *not*.

The Deep State is not the illuminati. It's not the Skull and

Bones. It's not the Freemasons. It's not some conspiracy theory. It's not some secret society pulling the strings of American politics. It's not a secret group that's hiding treasure and manipulating events according to some eternal scheme dreamed up by the super rich and powerful. It's not a quasi-sci-fi thriller that takes some great leap of faith to believe. It's not that complex. And it's not that far-fetched. It's real. In fact, it's quite simple to prove.

As lawyers, we deal in evidence. And right now we're going to make the case for how the Deep State is not only real, but is undermining the constitutional principles upon which America was founded, in order to subvert the conservative agenda.

Call it what you want: the Deep State, the Shadow Government, Obama holdovers, the out-of-control bureaucracy. It is composed of unelected, unaccountable government officials in positions of awesome power within our government who are using their authority to assert their will—not the people's will.

They are functioning, scheming, subverting, and undercutting the foundation of our democratic republic.

These really are the swamp creatures. The have spent their professional lives working in the federal government. They believe that government is the answer to all our ills. They believe that if the American people are wrong in how they vote, they can fix it through red tape and regulation (something we believe would be more aptly named "blue tape"). They are the worst of Washington, because they are deeply imbedded in the federal bureaucracy—the fourth branch of government that you won't find anywhere in the Constitution. They are not accountable to the people.

Yet they will stop at nothing to impose their subversive, radical, leftist ideology on you.

That's right, we the people voted. We made our opinion clear. And, in this great nation and time, where we get to choose our

"Caesar" by virtue of our vote, our vote is sacrosanct. It's special. We choose our government, or at least those who govern us.

We select the men and women who make the law, write the rules and regulations, seek justice in our courtrooms, guard our borders, and set the policy that will keep us safe and free—or not.

So it is not really that shocking, far-fetched, or extreme to recognize that the losers—who are not that used to losing—are trying to find a way to impose their will in spite of the choices we made on Election Day.

And, recognizing this reality, acknowledging this plainly demonstrable fact, is not radical. It's not fringe. And as long as they persuade us that our realization is "out there," that we're right-wing conspiracy theorists wearing tinfoil hats, we lose. They continue operating in the shadows, and the weight and revolutionary impact of our votes dissolve into political jargon.

We spoke. They don't like what we said. But we are in the right. Our vote has the force of law. The United States Constitution says so. Do you realize the weight of that? Do you understand how significant that is? We are in the right. We elected leaders. They—the Deep State—do not accept our choice. They think they know better. Their knowledge and wisdom transcends ours. They believe that. We, however, do not.

Their goal—expressly stated as #Resist—was to undermine the conservative agenda just long enough to take the House back—which they did—and then to try to take the Senate and the presidency—something we must not allow.

But our vote is not worth less than theirs just because they live and work inside the Beltway. That they work in the sea of cubicles up and down L'Enfant Plaza in the heart of Washington doesn't mean they understand American or world history better than we do. We'd say the contrary is true. Regardless, they still hold court between Independence, Constitution, and Pennsylvania Avenues in Washington. Making decisions. Funding the demise of their opponents. Selectively and strategically leaking information in their best effort to sway public opinion in their favor—and against ours.

You see, we elected a set of leaders in November 2016, in the White House and even on Capitol Hill, who promised us they would no longer play ball the way it had always been played before. The way it had always been was no longer acceptable. They promised us that. We believed them, and voted for a monumental shift in the Washington way. It was a political earthquake.

We voted to drain the swamp. How did you think the swamp creatures would react?

The Deep State thinks it knows better. They're here to temper our collective voice.

They retreated, so to speak, to the shadows, and gave birth to the Shadow Government. The establishment. The elite. #TheResistance.

It's not a conspiracy that requires some great level of faith to accept. It is real. And it is happening right in front of us.

Each day, headlines bring new proof. But before we get to some of these undeniable examples, just a quick note: this is not a book on the Deep State. My dad, Jay Sekulow, wrote that book already, *Undemocratic: Rogue, Reckless, and Renegade—How the Government is Stealing Democracy One Agency at a Time*. No, this is about the next red wave. But to achieve that, we must first understand who our adversaries are. And we must understand how dedicated they are to maintaining the old way, the establishment, their reign of repetitious bureaucracy. We must understand the significance of what they are doing to keep their power and place. We must understand what is truly at stake. The Deep State is thwarting our America. And we will suffer the consequences if we do nothing to stop them.

Think about it. The American people elected a president. There is no credible allegation or claim that anything about the 2016 presidential election was illegitimate. The electoral college results were overwhelmingly clear. But the candidate who won was not the one the Deep State wanted to win. He was not the candidate that they had selected. He was not the candidate that they had gone to great lengths to shield, protect, cover for, and usher into their predetermined seat of power.

So what could they do? Declare war. And declare war they did. It was not an actual war, mind you. It's more of an information war. Some call it a silent coup. Silence, shadows, conniving operatives buried deep in the foundations underneath the halls of our government. Secret efforts to bring down our elected leadership?

Is it really that hard to believe? It's real, people. Bureaucratic operatives. Holdovers from the Obama-Biden administration (even leftist ideologues going all the way back to the 1970s and the Carter administration) sitting in positions of power and influence that, unfortunately, seem unaffected by the change in political leadership imposed by our vote. In fact, it seems they've been mobilized *because* of our vote.

They are convinced that their candidate could never have lost in a fair fight. So, to them, there is no fair fight left. The ends justify the means. They stand resolute, willing to defy lawful executive orders and departmental policies and procedures. They are committed. Are we?

Here is the evidence—real-life examples of things that have happened. Indisputable things. We'll give you the inside story on what is happening, day in and day out, in Washington.

THE DEEP STATE AT WORK: A HISTORIC AND UNPRECEDENTED NUMBER OF LEAKS

The members of the Deep State have proven relentless in their efforts to impose their political will on the American people and the leadership we chose. One way the Deep State has waged its war on the Trump administration has been by leaking privileged, sensitive, and even classified government information. They are willing to do this all in an effort to stop the President, his White House, and his cabinet from succeeding in their agenda—an agenda that we, the American people, voted for.

The classified leaks, the violations of the Espionage Act, and the blatant lawlessness have become a rampant and repulsive danger to our republic.

Keep in mind that leaking certain types of information violates internal policies, rules, or regulations of the committee or agency holding those records. In some cases, leaking information is also a federal crime.

But that has not stopped the Deep State, which has engaged in nearly continual, "unprecedented"[1] leaks. In fact, in May 2017, the Senate Homeland Security and Governmental Affairs Committee released a report titled "State Secrets: How an Avalanche of Media Leaks Is Harming National Security."[2] It found that, up to that point, leaks were occurring at the *rate of one a day*," which was "seven times higher than the same period during the two previous administrations."

In the first 126 days of the Trump administration, there were at least 125 leaked stories from within the Deep State shadow government that were "potentially damaging to national security." That's a leak a day, every day, during a new president's most critical period—the first one hundred days of his or her administration.

During the same time period of the Bush and Obama administrations, the total number of combined leaks was only thirty-six. We knew the leaks were bad, but this is beyond the pale. It's astonishing and extremely dangerous to our national security.

The Senate report details:

The majority of leaks during the Trump administration, 78, concerned the Russia probes, with many revealing closely-held information such as intelligence community intercepts, FBI interviews and intelligence, grand jury subpoenas, and even the workings of a secret surveillance court.

Other leaks disclosed potentially sensitive intelligence on U.S. adversaries or possible military plans against them. One leak, about the investigation of a terrorist attack, caused a diplomatic incident between the United States and a close ally....

Federal law prohibits the unauthorized release of certain information that could damage our national security. The protection of our nation's secrets is essential to protecting intelligence activities, sources and methods, preserving the ability of the President to effectively achieve foreign policy objectives, and ultimately to safeguard our country. In short, the unauthorized disclosure of certain information can cost American lives, and our laws protecting this information provide for harsh punishments when violated. Since President Trump assumed office, our nation has faced an unprecedented wave of potentially damaging leaks of information protected by these important laws....

As *The New York Times* wrote in a candid self-assessment: "Journalism in the Trump era has featured a staggering number of leaks from sources across the federal government." No less an authority than President Obama's CIA director called the deluge of state secrets "appalling." These leaks do not occur in a vacuum. They can, and do, have real world consequences for national security. To ensure the security of our country's most sensitive information, federal law enforcement officials ought to thoroughly investigate leaks of potentially sensitive information flowing at an alarming rate.[3]

The Deep State is using the power of the United States government's intelligence apparatus as a weapon against the Left's political opponents. It's worse than the IRS targeting of conservatives, which we will explain in detail. It shows just how far the Deep State will go to impose its will. It has already shown that it is willing to violate federal law and endanger our national security in order to sabotage the conservative agenda. It is as shocking as it is dangerous. It must end.

The most astonishing leak came from fired FBI director James Comey. This leak is incredibly instructive on the attitude of the Deep State, whose proponents believe that they are above the law. Comey testified—under oath—that he intentionally leaked a privileged communication he had had with the President to the media through a friend in order to influence the Russia investigation. Read his words carefully: "My judgment was that I needed to get that out into the public square...because I thought that might prompt the appointment of a special counsel."[4] His judgment. Talk about bad judgment. That's right, Comey was resorting to leaking to try to influence the appointment of a special counsel.

The Deep State is taking such action each and every day in an attempt to undermine President Trump and the conservative agenda. It is repugnant to our republic, and it is crippling our Constitution.

DEEP STATE MUTINY

The Deep State mutiny takes on many forms. Remember former deputy attorney general Sally Yates? She was the most senior Obama holdover when President Trump first took office. As next in command, she was named as acting attorney general of the United States Department of Justice upon President Trump's inauguration.

The designation of an "acting" department head is routine. Someone has to hold the extremely important position of head of the Department of Justice until an incoming president names his or her own choice and that person is confirmed by the Senate.

Just as normal is the expectation that the person named to such a critical transitional office will faithfully fulfill the duties and obligations of that office without regard to political views or preferences. Perhaps more than at any other time, the nation needs consistency and order during the transition of power mandated by the American voters. The incoming administration needs to know that the operation of law enforcement and the implementation of national security will proceed unimpeded until the new leadership can take the helm.

This process makes America special. It is also part of what makes America great. The political parties in charge change. It is the peaceful transition of power that is unique to our system of government. But everyone, including politicians, the American people, and perhaps most important, America's enemies, have long been able to count on the baton changing hands smoothly. America's security—and much of the rest of the world's—will continue without a hitch. America's laws will be enforced.

Enter, the Deep State.

Yates had one job: hold the reins of the powerful Department of Justice until the new presidential administration selected its attorney general. Unsurprisingly, that job meant enforcing laws and rules both on the street and in the courtroom.

Yates, however, fancied herself as part of the "resistance." She and her cohorts, scattered throughout the federal government, saw themselves as smarter than the American voters. They knew better than us. They despised the candidate we'd chosen. And so, when the newly inaugurated president issued a lawful executive order that Yates did not like, an executive order based in the President's constitutional authority and in the authority expressly vested by Congress, Yates sprang into action.

Never mind that the executive order reflected a promise made by the President during the campaign. Never mind that, as Yates acknowledged, the Department of Justice's Office of Legal Counsel had deemed the order lawful in form and issuance. Never mind all that. She knew better. She sent her edict to the Department of Justice:

On January 27, 2017, the President signed an Executive Order regarding immigrants and refugees from certain Muslim-majority countries. The order has now been challenged in a number of jurisdictions. As the Acting Attorney General, it is my ultimate responsibility to determine the position of the Department of Justice in these actions.[5]

Note here Yates's own definition of her "ultimate responsibility," in which she left out her duty to enforce laws and maintain order. Undisturbed by such inconvenient and outdated notions, she continued, adding to her role the power to determine "whether any policy choice embodied in an Executive Order is wise or just." The shameless monologue went on:

Similarly, in litigation, DOJ Civil Division lawyers are charged with advancing reasonable legal arguments that can be made supporting an Executive Order. But my role as leader of this institution is different and broader. My responsibility is to ensure that the position of the Department of Justice is not only legally defensible, but is informed by our best view of what the law is after consideration of all the facts. In addition, I am responsible for ensuring that the positions we take in court remain consistent with this institution's solemn obligation to always seek justice and stand for what is right. At present, I am not convinced that the defense of the Executive Order is consistent with these responsibilities nor am I convinced that the Executive Order is lawful.

Consequently, for as long as I am the Acting Attorney General, the Department of Justice will not present arguments in defense of the Executive Order, unless and until I become convinced that it is appropriate to do so.[6]

Instead of being America's top lawyer—legally and ethically obligated to zealously represent her client, the United States and its laws, rules, regulations, and yes, executive orders—she appointed herself judge and jury—the final arbiter of the Constitution itself.

This is astounding. Outright rebellion. Mutiny at the very top of the nation's top law enforcement agency. Insubordination and defiance at what some commentators describe as the most sensitive time of our nation's existence—when a departing administration hands off power to an incoming administration. Even an opinion writer for the *Washington Post* exclaimed: "I am not aware of any instance in which the Justice Department has refused to defend a presumptively lawful executive action on this basis."[7] That same author went on to say that Yates should have resigned.

She was, fortunately, promptly terminated.[8]

But Yates's Deep State comrades hailed her as a hero. Andrew Weissmann, who was then a senior-level prosecutor in the department's Criminal Division and was a member of Special Counsel Robert Mueller's team investigating President Trump's campaign for supposed collusion with Russia, extolled Yates for her rebellion. "I am so proud," he gushed shortly after she issued her edict. "And in awe. Thank you so much. All my deepest respects."[9] And of course, leftist politicians, leftist academicians, and members of the mainstream media came to her defense, some of them calling her brave. She was even nominated for an award for courage.

This is outrageous. Backward. Up is now down. This, friends, is the Deep State.

Here's another example: On his way out the door, the director of the controversial Consumer Financial Protection Bureau (CFPB), Richard Cordray, attempted to appoint his replacement. He was resigning, yet he somehow thought he—and not the President—had the power to appoint the next CFPB director. He named Leandra English, who promptly anointed herself director. Following the Constitution, President Trump made his own appointment. English nevertheless ran out to the media claiming to be the rightful director (though she never showed up for work). She claimed a constitutional crisis, and even filed a lawsuit. That's right, a member of the Deep State filed a federal lawsuit against the President for making a presidential appointment that she didn't agree with. It was the Deep State that was creating a constitutional crisis. It's mind blowing.

Maybe the clearest window into the heart of the Deep State comes from the text messages between senior Comey-era FBI official Peter Strzok and his lover Lisa Page, who was also an FBI attorney. The tawdry affair is straight out of Hollywood, but you really can't make this stuff up. Numerous texts between the two discussed the establishment of a "secret society" within the FBI to oppose President Trump.

Another text described how senior FBI officials, including the number two at the FBI, Andrew McCabe, were working on an "insurance policy" were Trump to be elected president. Others showed their disdain for pro-life advocates—mostly young adults who were attending the annual pro-life rally in Washington called the March for Life—saying, "I truly hate these people," and cursing, "f***ing marchers." This barely scratches the surface of the Deep State.

Thankfully, none of these individuals remains in the federal bureaucracy, but they are just the tip of the iceberg.

Members of the Deep State have even been so bold as to write an op-ed in the pages of the *New York Times* entitled, "I Am Part of the Resistance Inside the Trump Administration," describing in detail how the Deep State is buried deep within the Trump administration with a goal to undermine his every policy.[10] It bears repeating: you cannot make this stuff up.

The Deep State is present everywhere in our government. Its members lurk in our law enforcement and intelligence agencies. They've been caught rigging climate results at the Environmental Protection Agency.[11] They account for the scandals inside the Veterans Administration[12] and the IRS. From leaks to cover-ups and corruption, from sham investigations of real crimes to sham investigations of no crimes at all, they press forward undeterred. You can be sure that they will not stop advancing their agenda; that they will resist any efforts to disinfect the system. Yes, these Deep State operators, these Obama administration holdovers embedded in agency offices and cubicles from L'Enfant Plaza to

Foggy Bottom, from the J. Edgar Hoover Building to the Harry S. Truman Building, and even all the way up to 1600 Pennsylvania Avenue, will continue to operate. They will continue their efforts to thwart the will of the American voter.

The only question is whether they will be identified, confronted, challenged (in court, if necessary), and held accountable to the law or the will of the American people. We will do everything in our power to bring the fight. But the American people have to rise to the occasion, too.

As we will show, we can win even in the midst of the most overwhelming corruption by the Deep State we have ever seen.

CHAPTER 5

CRASHING THE TEA PARTY

THE MOST INVIDIOUS EXAMPLE of the Deep State at work is the case of the IRS, which was implicated in one of the worst political targeting scandals of the century, and we were right there in the middle of it. The IRS systematically suffocated the movement that was responsible for the red wave of 2010—the Tea Party.

As we alluded to in our opening chapter, the IRS purposefully targeted conservative grassroots organizations that were attempting to oppose President Barack Obama's liberal agenda—perceiving them as a threat after their success at the ballot box in 2010 and in the run-up to his reelection efforts in 2012. Peaceful, lawful, constitutionally protected issue advocacy and opposition.

What they were doing was exercising their freedoms of speech and of assembly. These aren't found emanating from penumbras of the Bill of Rights. These are two of the first freedoms listed right there in the First Amendment. They aren't polite suggestions. They are inviolable edicts. They were earned by the blood, sweat, and tears of those who fought for our freedoms. Literally.

The irony is that it was revolutionary Americans who, in 1773, participated in the first tea party—the Boston Tea Party—and who secured the freedom that the members of the Tea Party sought to exercise.

Yet Tea Party organizations were targeted by the very government that had been established to protect the rights that they sought to exercise. Ironic, yes, and devastating to our democracy.

In a further irony, the Tea Party movement began as a response to President Obama's big government priorities, especially increased taxes and spending. Like its historical namesake, the Tea Party began as an uprising (though a far more peaceful one) by everyday Americans who were fed up with out-of-control government spending and taxation.

When it began, in 2009, the Tea Party was endlessly ridiculed by late-night TV hosts and the mainstream media alike. Its members were called nasty names like "teabaggers." They were relentlessly made fun of as conspiracy theorists, always claiming that the government was out to get them—that the IRS was out to get them.

The devastating irony was that they were right; the IRS was indeed bent on silencing them. The Left was trying to shut them down. The bureaucracy was trying to bury them in red/blue tape, to snuff them out, to suffocate their voices for freedom.

The Left—Obama-Biden loyalists, the Deep State bureaucracy, and the liberal, mainstream media—was afraid. The Tea Party was a true grassroots insurgency. It was "we the people."

In keeping with the theme that, to the Left, there is no such thing as a fair fight, the Deep State mobilized. When conservative groups across the country were organizing, so was the bureaucracy.

Remember, while we, concerned citizens trying to engage the political system, wield a force that comes from individual voters and groups who come together to convey messages to our peers and fellow countrymen, the government wields the blunt force of law. Government has the power of coercion. And what arm of the federal government has the reputation for being, perhaps, the most aggressive (and disliked) domestic manifestation of centralized, coercive government power? That's right. The IRS.

In one of the most famous Supreme Court cases of all time, *McCulloch v. Maryland*, Chief Justice John Marshall, paraphrasing the great orator Daniel Webster, said it best, "the power to tax involves the power to destroy...."[1]

Though he made that statement two hundred years ago, it remains applicable today. Destroy is exactly what the taxman set out to do to the fledgling Tea Party.

Deep State operatives from the IRS's rank and file all the way up to the top brass in Washington assembled and executed a nefarious plan.

You see, the Tea Party was not a political party at all. It was merely a grassroots organization of loosely—if at all—affiliated, civic-minded groups of everyday Americans who cared about the direction our nation was heading. They wanted a voice. So they formed associations. They met. They debated. They rallied around common, conservative goals. They did exactly what every civic textbook in the country says you're supposed to do. They did what the Constitution was established to protect. They engaged the political process. They exercised their civic duty.

And, like it or not, fledgling groups of any kind need one thing to survive and thrive: financial contributions. What did these groups need to attain before they could get those crucial contributions? Tax-exempt status.

And which government entity wields the awesome power to grant, deny, or ignore these groups' applications for that coveted status? That's right. The IRS.

Deep State operatives understand this. The swamp understands this. They understand, appreciate, and use the power they wield.

Unfortunately, by following the law, conservatives made their biggest "mistake." They filed numerous applications for tax-exempt status. They crossed every "t" and dotted every "i." The Deep State bureaucracy, on the other hand, did not. It directly violated the law, and it almost got away with it.

Here, the conservative groups were trying to implement their constitutional power. They were trying to stake out space on the political landscape. The only problem was that their adversaries held the power and might of the federal government's IRS.

And what did the IRS do? Did it wield its power with grace, dignity, class, and restraint? Did it apply the force of its regulatory might objectively and without regard to the political bent of the tax-exempt applicants' beliefs? Of course not.

Instead, it ignored the conservative groups' applications for tax-exempt status—until the conservative groups' applications, and hence their ability to fully engage the political process in opposition to the Left's champion (President Obama)—became moot.

Though many of our clients filed their applications for tax-exempt status between 2009 and 2012, they only recently began getting approved.

And another thing: the Left would have you believe these conservative groups were feeding off of foreign money; that they were super-sophisticated, super-rich organizations trying to play the system to make themselves even richer. They call it "dark money" or other scary-sounding names to make the Tea Party seem nefarious. This was not the case.

These organizations were "grassroots" in the truest sense of the word. They were ordinary Americans fed up with President

Obama's agenda and tactics. Tired of the lawlessness. Tired of the cover-ups. Tired of Washington. Tired of the swamp.

They were small business owners. Family men and women. Paying bills and raising kids—and worried about the out-of-control national debt, Obamacare, a depleted military. They were just normal, America-loving people who were scared about the direction President Obama and his Washington elites were taking the country—and the debilitating impact all of it would have on their children and grandchildren.

So they did what the law allowed and the U.S. Constitution protected: They grouped together to gain strength in numbers. They made sacrifices and did everything they knew to do in order to put their words and thoughts into action and to persuade their neighbors to do so as well.

But the Deep State Obama loyalists were one step ahead. And they controlled the government institutions whose favor and approval our clients would need.

The Left understood something that many other Americans don't. That is, they understood that if the conservative groundswell was prevented from gaining tax-exempt status for their groups, they would not garner enough political contributions to bring down the Left's champions—President Obama and certain key U.S. House and Senate seat holders who would prove critical in passing Obamacare. Without the all-important tax-exempt status, the conservatives could not sustain their messaging campaign. And so, while their message struck a chord with the American voter, it wasn't enough. They were silenced.

Our clients filed applications with the IRS, and waited. And waited. And the 2012 presidential and congressional elections came and went. And critical political races came and went. But our clients' applications for tax-exempt status just seemed to disappear into space.

In the law, we call this concept "irreparable harm." In a case where irreparable harm is successfully demonstrated, the court will issue an injunction, blocking the action (or in this case inaction) that is causing the harm, until the court has sufficient time to make what we call a "merits" decision—i.e., one based on evidence rather than technical or procedural grounds.

This legal and jurisprudential principle was meant to apply to situations where one party had all the time in the world and the other party had no time. In many lawsuits, one party has every reason to hold on as long as possible and let time pass. That party does not even need to "win" per se in the courtroom. If it can just run out the clock, that's just as good. And that is precisely what the IRS did.

Our clients, like so many others, lost something they can never get back. The IRS silenced them during pivotal national elections and policy debates, and that injustice can never be undone. Perhaps that's why the IRS never thought our clients would stand up and fight back. But fight back they did; this time in arenas all too often abandoned by our allied conservative causes—the courtroom and, maybe even more important in this case, the court of public opinion.

The IRS cases demonstrate a key principle that underlies our message in this book: when we're on the right side of the law, we can fight back—and win.

Here's how we did it:

In the early spring of 2012, we at the ACLJ began hearing from conservative organizations, Tea Party groups, and pro-life charities.

I remember the day we began taking those calls on our daily radio program, *Jay Sekulow Live.* No sooner did we put one or two on the air than we became inundated with calls. In hours, we had heard from dozens of these groups.

They all told a similar story: they had applied for tax-exempt status and the IRS either ignored them or asked horribly intrusive and burdensome questions. The IRS was demanding donor lists, membership lists, details about conversations group members participated in, meeting notes, and even the passwords to the groups' social media accounts. There were reports that the IRS even demanded of one group to know the "content of the members of your organization's prayers."[2] Talk about McCarthyism. It was insane.

If we hadn't actually gotten the demand letters that the IRS sent to these groups, no one would have believed them. They were not only absurd, but patently unconstitutional.

At the ACLJ, we went right to work representing these organizations. First, we told our clients to stop complying with these wholly unnecessary and in many cases unconstitutional document demands.

But some of our clients had already turned over sensitive information, including donor lists. If there is one thing Publius and the Federalist Papers taught us, it's that the First Amendment protects not only free speech but also anonymous speech. Alexander Hamilton's famous pseudonymous defense of our Constitution helped enshrine this critical type of free speech in the supreme law of our nation. It is what our nation was founded upon. The government doesn't get to know who is saying what.

Yet even those clients who had complied with the IRS's demand that they turn over hundreds of pages of their sensitive documents were being stonewalled. In fact, the IRS was asking them for even more.

It was utterly absurd.

The next thing we did was tell the IRS to go take a hike. In no uncertain terms, we let IRS officials know that their demands were wrong and that, until they started treating our clients fairly, they wouldn't get another of their documents.

For months, we battled with the IRS, which dragged its heels. Something just did not seem right.

Then came the day of reckoning. May 10, 2013. I will never forget it. News reports began to break that Lois Lerner, head of the Tax-Exempt Division of the IRS (who, until that day, almost *no one* had ever heard of) had just apologized for supposedly incidentally targeting hundreds of Tea Party groups. She tried to sweep it under the rug through a planted question at an American Bar Association meeting.

Here's what she said:

"We get about 60,000 applications for tax exemption every year, most of them are 501(c)(3) organizations. But between 2010 and 2012 we started seeing a very big uptick in the number of 501(c)(4) applications.... many of which indicated that they were going to be involved in advocacy work.

So **our line people** in Cincinnati who handled the applications did what we call centralization of these cases. They centralized work on these in one particular group. They do that for efficiency and consistency....

However, in these cases, the way they did the centralization **was not so fine**. Instead of referring to the cases as advocacy cases, they actually used case names on this list. **They used names like Tea Party or Patriots and they selected cases simply because the applications had those names in the title. That was wrong, that was absolutely incorrect, insensitive, and inappropriate**—that's not how we go about selecting cases for further review. We don't select for review because they have a particular name.

The other thing that happened was they also, in some

cases, **sat around for a while**. They also sent some letters out that were **far too broad**, asking questions of these organizations that weren't really necessary for the type of application. **In some cases you probably read that they asked for contributor names. That's not appropriate**, not usual, there are some very limited times when we might need that but in most of these cases where they were asked they didn't do it correctly and **they didn't do it with a higher level of review**. As I said, some of them **sat around for too long**.

What have we done to take care of this? Oh, let me back up. They didn't do this because of any political bias."[3]

Yes, let's do back up. You did what?!

She said it so nonchalantly that you would have thought she accidentally spilled some coffee on her desk.

As we were living out the headlines in these cases, this admission was jaw-dropping. What we soon realized was that Lerner's little stunt had been meticulously planned in order to get out ahead of an even worse report from the Treasury Inspector General for Tax Administration (TIGTA), which detailed widespread abuse against hundreds of conservative groups.

It was a full-blown scandal, and the IRS was in full-blown crisis-management mode.

Our response was simple: Apology not accepted. See you in court.

On May 28, 2013, the ACLJ filed our lawsuit, aptly captioned *Lynchpins of Liberty, et al. v. The United States of America, et al.*, against the IRS for wrongfully targeting our clients who, between 2009 and 2012, had tried to get their 501(c)(3) and (c)(4) tax-exempt status approved so they could compete for contributions from like-minded donors. We eventually represented forty-eight

Tea Party and conservative groups from twenty states in this federal litigation.

The truth finally began to come out about the IRS's actions—through congressional hearings, investigative reporting, public pressure from the ACLJ, and our lawsuit.

Yet the Left (including Lerner and President Obama himself) repeatedly and falsely claimed that the targeting of Tea Party and other conservative groups was merely the "boneheaded"[4] decision of a few rogue, low-level IRS agents located in Cincinnati. Remember, in Lerner's original so-called apology, she called them "our line people in Cincinnati." They threw those agents in Cincinnati under the bus and insisted that the main IRS office, in Washington, had nothing to do with it. According to Obama, there had not been even a "smidgen of corruption" in what the IRS did.[5]

It seems the swamp defines "corruption" differently than the rest of us, because despite their protestations of innocence, emails uncovered a year into our lawsuit from senior IRS officials *in Washington* proved otherwise.

In fact, we obtained demand letters signed by Lerner herself requiring Tea Party groups to provide to the IRS obtrusive information from our clients. So much for Lerner's assertion that "they didn't do it with a higher level of review."

What's more, while these emails made headlines, much of the news media missed a critical point, the "smoking gun": Conservatives weren't just targeted by the IRS. Washington wasn't just sort of indirectly involved. No, Washington had directed the targeting—from the beginning.

Within twenty-four hours of the first Tea Party case being "flagged" in early 2010, senior IRS officials under Lerner's command in Washington took control of the situation and began their calculated scheme to silence the opposition, KGB-style.

They employed the full force and power of perhaps the most feared arm of the United States government, the IRS, to shut down conservatives.

The facts of this case were complicated. The facts underlying cases of corruption often are. We must be willing to take the time and devote the resources necessary to peel back the onion. That's because understanding the initial sequence of events is the key to understanding how high-level IRS officials in Washington intentionally directed the targeting of these groups. The following is a timeline of the events that we first published in the *Washington Times* as we uncovered the evidence in May 2014:[6]

Feb. 25, 2010: In an email chain between senior IRS officials in Washington and field offices in Cincinnati and California titled, "High Profile Case—Does [Exempt Organizations (EO)] Technical Want It?" Holly Paz, who would later become Lerner's deputy in Washington, was made aware that a "potentially politically embarassing [sic] case involving a 'Tea Party' organization" had been flagged. By the next morning, Paz had requested that it be sent to Washington, "given the potential for media interest."

March 16–17, 2010: The same email chain, now titled "High Profile Case—EO Technical Would Like It," continues, with Paz acknowledging that she had "one Tea Party case up here" and instructing Cincinnati to send "a few more cases" to Washington and to "hold the rest." That line was key. Paz, from Washington, clearly instructed the Cincinnati IRS office that Washington would be responsible for future Tea Party cases, stating, "we will work with [Cincinnati] in working the other cases." The chain continues with senior IRS officials in Cincinnati and California confirming their implementation of Washington's orders to "hold" the "Tea Party cases."

April 23, 2010: Steven Grodnitzky, the acting manager of EO Technical, directly below Paz in Washington, instructed his staff to create an "SCR [Sensitive Case Report] for the Tea Party cases." He further instructed senior IRS officials in Cincinnati and California that his office in Washington was working on the first "2 Tea Party cases" and that their offices should "coordinate" with his office and set up "a call" before developing the rest of the cases. Emails over the next few days between Grodnitzky in Washington and IRS officials in Cincinnati and California, under the subject line "Tea Party Cases," show that coordination being put in place.

July 6, 2010: Paz instructed Grodnitzky to follow up with the IRS teams in Cincinnati and California and remind them "we have been handling Tea Party applications the last few months." Grodnitzky, again from Washington, reiterated the instructions, "[Exempt Organizations Technical in Washington] is working the Tea Party applications in coordination with Cincy....Because the Tea Party applications are the subject of an SCR, we cannot resolve any of the cases without coordinating with Rob." "Rob" is presumably Rob Choi, who was then director of rulings and agreements in Washington, directly below Lerner. It was Paz who replaced Choi as Lerner's deputy in December 2010.

From there, we know the applications of conservative groups were held for two more years, until senior IRS officials in Washington, including the IRS chief counsel's office, developed unconstitutionally intrusive demand letters, and began sending them out in early 2012.

This was nothing less than iron-fisted intimidation by political hacks convinced they are above the law. This is abuse of power. This is corruption. It's a manifestation of the Deep State.

It's clear, too, that they believed they could get away with it. But that's where we got involved.

At the ACLJ, we began receiving contacts from numerous conservative groups in March 2012 about these unconstitutionally intrusive IRS demand letters—including demands for donor lists and other impermissible information requests. They came from IRS offices in Cincinnati, California, and Washington, D.C., and included some signed by Lerner herself. After stalling for another year, the IRS admitted irregularities and issued its so-called apology in May 2013, but intentionally withheld the large role played by the D.C. headquarters. It was not until more than four years later that all of our clients received a determination from the IRS regarding their tax-exempt status—*with one organization in particular waiting for over seven years.*

That's why, just days after Lerner. and the IRS's so-called apology, the ACLJ filed a massive lawsuit against the IRS for implementation of an unlawful targeting scheme whereby the IRS singled out the applications of conservative organizations, delayed processing those applications, then made harassing, probing, and unnecessary requests for additional information that often required applicants to disclose, among other things: donor lists, communications with members of legislative bodies, internet passwords and usernames, and political and charitable activities of officers and their family members.

In October 2014, the district court dismissed our claims and concluded that the IRS had voluntarily ceased all unlawful conduct. Undeterred, we appealed that decision to the U.S. Court of Appeals for the D.C. Circuit, and prevailed. In August 2016, the federal appellate court reversed the district court's decision. The appellate court found that the IRS had failed to meet its burden showing that either (1) the targeting scheme or (2) its effects on our clients in the case had actually ended. After that, the case went back down to the district court, where we succeeded in getting the IRS to hand over evidence to us (discovery). This ultimately led to the IRS being required to give an account for its conduct.

And, through our case, we learned that the command to "hold" the conservatives' applications came straight from Washington beginning in 2010; it continued in 2014; and it was not fully exposed and dealt with until October of 2017. For these years, the Obama-Biden administration successfully stonewalled and deflected attention from the truth. The fact that the administration intentionally and falsely insisted to the American people that these direct orders did not come from the heart of the bureaucratic Deep State in Washington means that the cover-up was as much a part of the scandal as the targeting had been in the first place.

Documents released in our lawsuit revealed that the Obama IRS created a special group to review "all applications associated with the Tea Party." The goal of the special group was to ensnare targeted organizations' tax exemption applications and hamper their ability to affect the 2012 elections. The Deep State had seen the red wave these groups helped start in 2010 and wanted to stop it from happening again. These conservative organizations, including our clients, were placed on "Be-on-the-Lookout" (BOLO) lists if their names or policy positions appeared to be affiliated with the Tea Party.

Their applications were all shipped off to a special group at the IRS. It was tax-exempt purgatory. Never to be heard from again. Until we came along.

Throughout that time, the IRS had been able to protect its political targeting scheme by hiding its operations and activity behind the layers of bureaucracy festering within the agency. But it also got help and cover by cooperating with other government agencies under the Obama administration.

ALPHABET SOUP OF CORRUPTION

In the summer of 2015, the story broke that Lerner and the IRS were colluding with President Obama's FBI and DOJ to bring false charges against the conservative groups the IRS was already unlawfully targeting. When the story broke, we called it an "alphabet soup of corruption." That was because the IRS, FBI, and DOJ had been exposed attempting to target and prosecute political opponents.

Thus it was no surprise to us when the FBI and DOJ became embroiled in political corruption charges in 2016 and 2017. We had seen it before.

Documents revealed through a Freedom of Information Act (FOIA) lawsuit filed by our friends at Judicial Watch showed that several IRS officials, including Lerner, colluded with the FBI and DOJ to develop "several possible theories to bring criminal charges" against conservative groups as early as 2010—which not coincidentally was around the time the IRS operatives had begun flagging the groups' applications for tax-exempt status.

On July 7, 2015, the *Washington Free Beacon* reported the story:

Newly obtained documents from the conservative educational foundation Judicial Watch detail an official memo from October 2010 of a meeting between Lois Lerner and officials at the Department of Justice and the FBI to plan for the prosecution of targeted nonprofit organizations.

A lawsuit filed under the Freedom of Information Act produced the documents which included the memo as well as revelations that the Justice Department wanted IRS employees to turn over sensitive documents before giving them to Congress, Judicial Watch said in a press release....

An IRS document confirms that the organization supplied

the FBI with 21 computer disks containing 1.25 million pages of confidential information from more than 113,000 tax returns.[7]

Remember all those unconstitutional and obtrusive demands for information our clients got from the IRS, and some of them complied with? Well, that information was then shipped off to the FBI.

Notes from this high-level, October 8, 2010, meeting showed that Lerner and several other IRS officials "met with the section chief and other attorneys from the Department of Justice Criminal Division's Public Integrity Section, and one representative from the FBI, to discuss recent attention to the political activity of exempt organizations." Shockingly, those discussions focused on "several possible theories to bring criminal charges" against these conservative groups.[8]

This level of collusion among the IRS, FBI, and DOJ—at a time when conservative groups were being targeted for their political beliefs by Lerner's division of the IRS—is ridiculous and appalling. But it is not surprising. What's worse, Lerner and the DOJ continued these conversations for years. Nearly three years later—two days before Lerner issued her faux apology for having targeted conservatives—Lerner wrote an email to the chief of staff for the acting commissioner of the IRS explaining ongoing discussions with senior DOJ officials to "**piece together false statement cases about applicants.**"[9]

That's right, two days before her so-called apology, Lerner was still colluding with the DOJ to "piece together" false charges against the very Tea Party groups the IRS was unlawfully targeting. Again, sound familiar—similar to another DOJ investigation to piece together politically motivated, false charges? No one has to "piece together" legitimate charges. To "piece together" is just a nice way of saying you are trying to make something up. There was nothing nice about it.

These revelations led to only one conclusion. Stopping the conservatives from getting the tax-exempt status they deserved by violating their constitutionally protected speech and association rights was not enough. No, Lerner and her allies throughout the Obama-Biden administration wanted to throw the conservative opposition in jail.

This is sickening. It's a grave abuse of our justice system—one we have again seen rear its ugly head. It's right out of the Deep State's playbook.

It's as if these revelations were ripped from the pages of a George Orwell novel. But this isn't fiction.

The Left, wielding the blunt instruments of the IRS, DOJ, and FBI, was hitting conservatives from every angle.

As we said then, Washington orchestrated it; Washington directed it; and no amount of Obama administration spin could change that fact. We, on behalf of our clients and others, stayed on the front lines until the IRS was held accountable. The integrity of the First Amendment and free speech in the United States was at stake.

And it was not until a change in leadership in Washington, *imposed by the American voter*—another red wave—that the accountability we desperately needed came to pass. President Trump's leadership, through the vehicle of our federal lawsuit and others, righted the wrong.

VICTORY

In a consent order agreed to by the parties and entered by the court on December 11, 2017, the IRS apologized for its treatment of our clients during the tax-exempt determinations process. The IRS had denied its corruption and wrongdoing for years. But now, it expressly admitted to us and a federal court that the way it treated the conservative groups we represented was wrong.

This is what the order said:

> The IRS admits that its treatment of Plaintiffs during the tax-exempt determinations process, including screening their applications based on their names or policy positions, subjecting those applications to heightened scrutiny and inordinate delays, and demanding of some Plaintiffs' information that TIGTA [Treasury Inspector General for Tax Administration] determined was unnecessary to the agency's determination of their tax-exempt status, was wrong. For such treatment, the IRS expresses its sincere apology.

The order went on to bar the IRS from ever again engaging in politically motivated targeting against conservative groups. That's an enforceable court order. If it happens again, we can take that court order right back to the judge.

This order marked the end of a four-year legal battle initiated by the ACLJ on behalf of numerous conservative organizations targeted by the IRS solely because of their political viewpoints and the threat they posed to the ruling party then in power.

Our objective from the very beginning had been to hold the IRS accountable for its discrimination, intimidation, falsehoods, and corruption. And we won.

Now the IRS is bound by new rules prohibiting the kind of corrupt conduct it got away with for so long. Lerner and others were chastised and lost their jobs. Our clients were vindicated. The IRS was exposed and its officials were embarrassed. And, as these lawsuits progressed, and as pressure from us, Congress, and the general public intensified, the public outrage that ensued undoubtedly played a role in turning the tide and bringing about the red wave in the 2016 presidential and congressional elections. This case put government corruption in the spotlight, and kept it there. We, the American people, had had enough.

This order marked a historic victory for our clients and it sent a message loud and clear that we will not allow a government agency to target conservative organizations, or any organizations for that matter, because of their political viewpoints. This order, and the years of litigation it represents, sends the message that when we fight back, we can win.

Our clients' courage and commitment in this case, and the courage and commitment of numerous others, resulted in this order putting the IRS in its place. This will end the IRS's fascist behavior against our clients, as the IRS has expressly acknowledged that what it did was "wrong." It even included a real apology!

But we got more than that. We got an enforceable court order. And, in addition to our main lawsuit, the IRS in April 2018 awarded more than $3.5 million in a settlement to the more than four hundred Tea Party groups it had targeted.

The victors included our clients.

As part of the settlement, then–Attorney General Jeff Sessions made clear: "There is no excuse for this conduct.... Hundreds of organizations were affected by these actions, and they deserve an apology from the IRS."[10] We helped make the IRS pay for what they had done.

While the agreements and order we secured are designed to prevent this from happening again, we must and will remain vigilant to keep the IRS in check.

It's true that we could not undo the corruption and the irreparable harm the IRS caused not just to our clients, but to the nation as a whole. We couldn't undo the far-reaching impact the IRS's silencing had on critical conservative grassroots movements and political elections. But we could fight back. We could stand up and defend the rights of our clients and the rule of law.

And while nothing is impossible in Washington, this case and the victory we won will make it much harder for IRS bureaucrats to abuse their power again in the same way. As we said, new policies have been put in place as a result of this case. The federal court is watching, and now Deep State holdovers embedded in the IRS are on notice that any attempt to pull these kinds of stunts again will violate a federal court order. Now the kind of corruption they got away with in the shadows for seven years stands exposed in the light.

It may be true that we can never fully stop corruption in our government. But we can beat it back. We can fight it, and we can win.

Here's how we know the difference our case made: **"They've been burned. They've been hammered. They've been bludgeoned,"** George Washington University law professor and nonprofit law expert Miriam Galston told the *Washington Post* in response to a question about the impact our lawsuit had on the IRS. **"They're trying to survive."**[11]

Here's our free advice to the IRS: Stop the corruption and maybe your survival will get easier. We'll never stop holding you accountable.

CHAPTER 6

THE DEEP STATE SWAMP FESTERS AS THE VIRUS OF DECEPTION SPREADS

AS THE IRS CASES show, the Deep State is not new. It was around during and even before the Obama administration. But the eight years of the Obama-Biden administration hid its impact. It was growing, entrenching. We are only now seeing the massive and undeniable effects of the Deep State.

As the IRS case began to wind down, we began to see other impacts from the Deep State, and the IRS cases and our experience fighting that burgeoning bureaucratic behemoth gave us insight into how to defeat it.

The next red wave requires that we drain the swamp.

The first step is to expose the corruption. We set out to do just that and found the Deep State swamp festering with lies. It was a virus of deception.

At the ACLJ, we file numerous lawsuits against the Deep State—against agencies and departments that continually, and unabashedly, flout the law. We've uncovered some unbelievable corruption through our legal demands and lawsuits against the federal bureaucracy. Some of our lawsuits have made headlines. Others, however, have not. Through each, we have exposed how the Deep State is willing to undermine the very Constitution of the United States in its attempt to thwart the conservative agenda.

DEEP STATE DELETES VIDEO TO HIDE OBAMA'S IRAN DEAL LIE

We'll start with an example from the Obama State Department, and its brazen attempt to hide when the Obama-Biden administration began secret bilateral talks with Iran that resulted in the Iran Nuclear Deal (formally entitled the Joint Comprehensive Plan of Action, or JCPOA). Remember, Iran was then and remains today the number one state sponsor of terrorism in the world. Remember, too, that the Obama administration's Iran deal was extremely controversial and unpopular. In response, the Obama administration generated talking points and positions defending its efforts to secure the deal.

One of those talking points was that the Obama administration had waited to negotiate the Iran deal until the allegedly less extreme Iranian regime had taken power in Iran in 2013, with the election of Hassan Rouhani as president.[1] This was a key point that the Obama administration pushed in its efforts to gain support for the deal and respond to criticism that the United States ought not be negotiating with Iran's undeniably extreme and anti-American leadership.

Fox News's chief Washington correspondent at the time, James Rosen, directly confronted the Obama State Department and knocked down the first domino that led to the exposure of the agency's lie—and just how far it would go to keep it hidden from the American people. Here's what happened:

On May 9, 2016, Rosen reported that the Obama State Department had deleted part of the video of its daily press briefing—from all the way back on December 2, 2013.[2] The deletion removed approximately eight minutes of video. What was in the deleted portion of the video? Why was it deleted? Well, it contained a series of questions raised by Rosen about when the Obama administration actually began its talks with Iran, and answers to those questions from State Department spokeswoman Jen Psaki.

Specifically, Rosen asked Psaki what year the Obama administration began its direct secret talks with Iran that led to the deal. At the daily press briefing on December 2, 2013, Rosen asked Psaki if the talks had begun in 2011, as Deputy National Security Adviser Ben Rhodes had recently told the *New York Times*.[3]

Here's what was deleted from the video, but was discovered in the State Department's transcript:

QUESTION: On the sixth of February in this room, I had a very brief exchange with your predecessor, Victoria Nuland—

MS. PSAKI: Mm-hmm.

QUESTION: —about Iran. And with your indulgence, I will read it in its entirety for the purpose of the record and so you can respond to it.

"Rosen: There have been reports that intermittently, and outside of the formal P5+1 mechanisms, the Obama Administration, or members of it, have conducted direct secret bilateral talks with Iran. Is that true or false?"

"Nuland: We have made clear, as the vice president did at Munich, that in the context of the larger P5+1 framework, we would be prepared to talk to Iran bilaterally. But with regard to the kind of thing that you're talking about on a government-to-government level, no."

That's the entirety of the exchange.[4]

71

Mr. Rosen continued:

QUESTION: As we now know, senior state department officials had, in fact, been conducting direct, secret bilateral talks with senior officials of the Iranian Government in Oman, *perhaps dating back to 2011 by that point.* So the question today is a simple one: When the briefer was asked about those talks and flatly denied them from the podium, that was untrue, correct?

MS. PSAKI: I mean, James, I—that—you're talking about a February briefing, so 10 months ago. I don't think we've outlined or confirmed contacts or specifics beyond a March meeting. I'm not going to confirm others beyond that at this point. So I don't know that I have any more for you.

QUESTION: Do you stand by the accuracy of what Ms. Nuland told me, that there had been no government-to-government contacts, no secret direct bilateral talks with Iran as of the date of that briefing, February 6th? Do you stand by the accuracy of that?

MS. PSAKI: James, I have no new information for you today on the timing of when there were any discussions with any Iranian officials.

QUESTION: Let me try it one last way, Jen—

MS. PSAKI: Okay.

QUESTION: —and I appreciate your indulgence.

MS. PSAKI: Sure.

QUESTION: *Is it the policy of the State Department, where the preservation or the secrecy of secret negotiations is concerned, to lie in order to achieve that goal?*

MS. PSAKI: *James, I think there are times where diplomacy needs privacy in order to progress. This is a good example of that.* Obviously, we have made clear and laid out a number of details in recent weeks about discussions and about a bilateral channel that fed into the P5+1 negotiations, and we've answered questions on it, we've confirmed details. We're happy to continue to do that, but clearly, this was an important component leading up to the agreement that was reached a week ago.

QUESTION: Since you, standing at that podium last week, did confirm that there were such talks, at least as far back as March of this year, I don't see what would prohibit you from addressing directly this question: *Were there secret direct bilateral talks between the United States and Iranian officials in 2011?*

MS. PSAKI: I don't have anything more for you today. We've long had ways to speak with the Iranians through a range of channels, some of which you talked—you mentioned, but I don't have any other specifics for you today.

QUESTION: One more on Iran?

QUESTION: The *Los Angeles Times* and *Politico* have reported that those talks were held as far back as 2011. Were those reports inaccurate?

MS. PSAKI: I'm not sure which reports you're talking about. Are you talking about visits that the Secretary and others made to Oman, or are you talking about other reports?

QUESTION: I'm talking about U.S. officials meeting directly and secretly with Iranian officials in Oman as far back as 2011. The *Los Angeles Times* and *Politico* have reported those meetings. Were those reports inaccurate?

MS. PSAKI: I have nothing more for you on it, James, today.[5]

Additional video footage that was deleted contained dialogue between Psaki and Rosen that highlighted another embarrassing fact for the Obama administration. Back when the Iran deal was announced, then–Secretary of State John Kerry had conducted a series of media interviews in Geneva, Switzerland. Part of his presentation included a talking point to this effect: When Tehran had reached out to the Bush-Cheney administration in 2003, Iran possessed just 164 centrifuges. According to Kerry, speaking in July 2015, Iran had 19,000 centrifuges, and so the deal was the best possible deal that could be had. In other words, he suggested that much of Iran's nuclear capability growth had occurred under Bush-Cheney and that the great Obama-Biden administration was saving the day by stopping the bleeding, so to speak.

But that scenario fell apart under Rosen's questioning. "Isn't it a fact that since the Obama-Biden Administration took office, 70 percent of Iran's centrifuges have been installed?" he asked.

Psaki's response? "Well, I'd have to look at the statistics, James, but we have not questioned the fact that Iran has made progress on enrichment and on developing a nuclear weapon. We have not questioned that."[6]

Psaki's response was not a denial. And it further reveals how dishonest and slick the Obama State Department was. Unsurprisingly, this discussion was also deleted from the daily press briefing video that day:

> *MS. PSAKI:* That's one of the reasons why we stepped up sanctions over the past couple of years. The President and Secretary Kerry were big proponents of that. We worked with the international community to do just that to put that necessary pressure in place.[7]

According to a *Fox News* piece on the deletion, it "was missing from the department's official website and its YouTube channel. The department now says it cannot explain the deletion and is working to restore the material."[8] However, as of May 10, 2016, when we were preparing our FOIA request,[9] the full, unedited video was available on the State Department's website.[10] Yet the edited version, as of May 10, 2016, remained on the U.S. State Department's YouTube channel.[11]

That same day, then-senior-level State Department spokeswoman Elizabeth Trudeau claimed the deletion of part of the video "was a glitch" and again that "genuinely we think it was a glitch."[12]

The deletion was obvious. Just as obvious to any novice in audiovisual technology as it was that the deletion was no glitch. The white flash, a known editing tool in video production whereby a brief flash of light is inserted where an edit is made in a video as a transition, gave it away.

That is when we decided to get involved by engaging a critical legal process made available by the Freedom of Information Act (FOIA). This law provides the right for American citizens to request records, notes, emails, etc., from the various agencies of the executive branch, and it requires those agencies to disclose the requested records within a certain amount of time. There are, of course, some exceptions, but generally, the law is pretty clear about what the agencies have to do to comply. We decided to use this process to see if we could find out what had really happened—to see if the Obama State Department was telling the truth, or whether we were witnessing the Deep State at work. We had a feeling we knew the answer.

Here are some examples of what we requested:

- Records reflecting the names of any and all State Department officials, their staffs, any person conducting the meeting or briefing, or any other persons present at any meeting or briefing at which any State Department official or their staff discussed the content of the video recording of the daily press briefing, December 2, 2013, that was deleted, edited, altered, or otherwise manipulated.

- Records containing any discussion that any portion of the video recording should be deleted, edited, altered, or otherwise manipulated.
- Records containing any discussion, instruction, direction, order, command, or suggestion that any portion of the video recording be deleted, edited, altered, or otherwise manipulated.

Not long after we sent our FOIA request to the State Department, a spokesman for the agency admitted what we knew all along, that the deletion of a key portion of this briefing was not a "glitch," as the State Department had first claimed. No, the deletion was intentional. In fact, State Department spokesman Admiral John Kirby later admitted that "a specific request was made to excise that portion of the briefing."[13]

He went on to explain the official position of the department: "We do not know who made the request to edit the video, or why it was made.... There were no rules in place at the time to govern this sort of action, so while I believe it was an inappropriate step to take, I see little foundation for pressing forward with a formal investigation."[14]

That was ridiculous. As we said at the time, the Obama administration had lied to us—the American people—about the most critical diplomatic negotiations in decades. We deserved answers. This is when we decided we would do whatever it took to get them—and to insist that the State Department comply with the FOIA requirements and provide them. We filed our FOIA request on behalf of nearly 150,000 Americans who had signed our petition to expose the truth about the Iran lie.

We were surprised at the State Department's initial response to our FOIA request. They sent us a short, vague letter that obviously did not satisfy their obligations under the law. And so, when the twenty-business-day deadline passed and we had received nothing else—no more letters, no records, nothing—we took it to the next level. We took the State Department to federal court in Washington.

In our lawsuit against the Obama State Department, we received definitive evidence that the Obama-Biden administration deliberately manipulated the public video record of a press briefing—deleting a portion in which it admitted lying to the American people about the Iran nuclear negotiations.

After months of arduous litigation efforts, we finally got the smoking gun.

We forced the State Department to turn over what the department had labeled a "sensitive but unclassified" internal review of the matter. The evidence of deception was unmistakable. The State Department's internal review memo contained a section called: "Evidence of Purposeful Editing."[15]

This review showed that the State Department's own internal records reveal that a technician in its Bureau of Public Affairs (PA) "received a request to edit the video over the phone from a female caller from elsewhere in PA who could credibly assert that an edit should be made."[16] Moreover, the document provides definitive testimony that "the requester had mentioned in the course of the call a Fox network reporter and Iran. The technician indicated that the requester may also have provided the start and end times for an edit."[17]

This is astounding. Equally astounding, perhaps, is the fact that the State Department announced that it would not follow up on the investigation or take any punitive action against anyone involved.[18] They just swept it under the rug.

This was the clearest evidence to date that the Obama State Department, through its unelected Deep State collaborators embedded within the agency, intentionally edited the video and deleted this critical exchange from the public video record. They got caught and tried to cover it up. We helped uncover it.

As in most of our FOIA cases, many, many pages of the documents the State Department ended up providing to us were heavily redacted. We are certain that most of these redactions are not valid and that, instead, they are just covering up conversations that, if made public, would further embarrass the Obama-Biden administration. As in all our FOIA cases, we have challenged these redactions, raising our objections to the court. We'll keep pressing forward.

Our legal efforts to force the State Department to hand over its records so that the American people could find out what really happened helped us shine a public light on the duplicitous Iran deal, and the Obama administration's secretive and manipulative tactics to protect it at a critical time—leading up to the American presidential election. While many issues contributed to the red wave of 2016—the American people's decision to fundamentally change the direction of its leadership in Washington—this issue was one of them.

Since then, President Trump has withdrawn the United States from the disastrous—and deceptive—Iran deal and reimposed many of the sanctions that President Obama had lifted on the world's leading state sponsor of terrorism. But to defeat the deal, we first had to expose the deception.

This fact demonstrates a central point we want to underscore. We, the American people, the authors of this book, the professionals at the American Center for Law and Justice, do not hold an office in the government or possess the power of law enforcement. We cannot bring criminal proceedings against wrongdoers. We are not prosecutors. But there is much we can do. We must identify all that we can do, and do it. Action is the key.

THE DEEP STATE IN ITS PRIME: URANIUM ONE

The Deep State has long operated unchecked in the mazes of bureaucracy where deals are done and money is made. This is the story of the Clintons and Uranium One.

In 2010, the Obama administration approved the sale of control over 20 percent of America's uranium production capacity to an energy conglomerate known as Rosatom, which was owned and controlled by the Russian government. The prize was Uranium One, a Canadian mining company over which Rosatom had obtained total control three years later. That gave the Russians control over a large portion of America's uranium, a strategic nuclear resource. How could such a significant transaction have been allowed to occur? Well, there were Clintons involved.

The Committee on Foreign Investments in the United States (CFIUS) was the machinery they used to make it happen. This committee approved the deal, giving the Russian government control over American uranium. The committee comprises the heads and staffs of multiple agencies of the federal government. One of those is the U.S. Department of State, which just so happened to be headed at the time by Hillary Clinton, who was then secretary of state.

In the time leading up to the committee's approval of the deal, the FBI was investigating bribes, kickbacks, and racketeering by the Russian conglomerate's American subsidiary that were calculated to compromise contractors in the American nuclear energy industry.[19] CFIUS would have known this because the attorney general's representative sat on the committee. Unbelievably, at the same time, Russian nuclear officials, "those linked to Uranium One or UrAsia," another company involved in the series of transactions at issue, had reportedly given $145 million to the Clinton Foundation.[20] What's more, then-Secretary Clinton's husband received $500,000 from the Russian government via "a regime-tied Russian bank" for a speech in Moscow.[21]

Let's examine this a bit closer. First, the Obama administration approved a deal that transferred 20 percent of American uranium production capacity to a Russian-owned energy conglomerate. That in and of itself is outrageous. And, prior to the approval of that deal, the FBI had collected "substantial evidence" that the Russian nuclear industry, operated by the Russian government, "had compromised an American uranium trucking firm with bribes and kickbacks in violation of the Foreign Corrupt Practices Act."[22] The head of the FBI's leading oversight agency, the Department of Justice, sat on CFIUS and did not block the deal.

And, according to the *Hill*, the FBI "obtained an eyewitness account—backed by documents—indicating Russian nuclear officials had routed millions of dollars to the U.S. designed to benefit former President Bill Clinton's charitable foundation during the time Secretary of State Hillary Clinton served on a government body that provided a favorable decision to Moscow."[23]

So Hillary Clinton, as secretary of state, sat on the committee that approved the transfer of a controlling interest in Uranium One to Russian state-owned ARMZ—a wholly owned subsidiary of the Russian nuclear giant Rosatom. And this happened in the same committee on which the Department of Justice, which was investigating corruption of relevant actors, also sat.

This was no small transaction. The *New York Times* reported that the "deal made Rosatom one of the world's largest uranium producers and brought [Russian President Vladimir] Putin closer to his goal of controlling much of the global uranium supply chain."[24] These are not just our words. The *New York Times* continued:

The untold story behind that story is one that involves not just the Russian president, but also a former American president and a woman who would like to be the next one.

At the heart of the tale are several men, leaders of the Canadian mining industry, who have been major donors to the charitable endeavors of former President Bill Clinton and his family. Members of that group built, financed and eventually sold off to the Russians a company that would become known as Uranium One.

Beyond mines in Kazakhstan that are among the most lucrative in the world, the sale gave the Russians control of one-fifth of all uranium production capacity in the United States. Since uranium is considered a strategic asset, with implications for national security, the deal had to be approved by a committee composed of representatives from a number of United States government agencies. Among the agencies that eventually signed off was the State Department, then headed by Mr. Clinton's wife, Hillary Rodham Clinton.

As the Russians gradually assumed control of Uranium One in three separate transactions from 2009 to 2013, Canadian records show, a flow of cash made its way to the Clinton Foundation.[25]

Newsweek reported that the Clinton Foundation received $145 million from "those linked to Uranium One or UrAsia."[26] Let that sink in.

But wait, there's more. The *National Review* reported:

In March 2010, to push the Obama "reset" agenda, Secretary Clinton traveled to Russia, where she met with Putin and Dimitri Medvedev.... Soon after, it emerged that Renaissance Capital, a regime-tied Russian bank, had offered Bill Clinton

$500,000 to make a single speech—far more than the former president's usual haul in what would become one of his biggest paydays ever. Renaissance was an aggressive promoter of Rosatom. The Clinton speech took place in Moscow in June.[27]

And it gets worse. According to reporting by the *National Review*, "at the time the administration approved the transfer, it knew that Rosatom's American subsidiary [Tenam USA] was engaged in a lucrative racketeering enterprise that had already committed felony extortion, fraud, and money-laundering offenses" as part of a concerted effort to "compromise[] the American companies that paid the bribes, rendering players in U.S. nuclear energy—a sector critical to national security—vulnerable to blackmail by Moscow."[28] Tenam USA itself was never charged, but its former president, Vadim Makerin, would later plead guilty to conspiracy to commit money laundering in violation of federal law.[29]

It is clear that something bad happened. What is not clear is just how much information about the Russian nuclear corruption was provided by the FBI or the Department of Justice to the members of CFIUS. It's also unclear why Russian nuclear officials were allowed to route millions of dollars to the Clinton Foundation while then–Secretary of State Clinton was sitting on the committee that then approved a transaction that gave the Russians control of one-fifth of U.S. uranium production capacity. Talk about Russian collusion.

The Deep State hides in the shadows, so we have to flush them out. That is precisely why we, at the ACLJ, sent FOIA requests to the Department of the Treasury, the Department of State, the Department of Justice and its National Security Division, and the FBI—all key members of the committee that approved the deal. We sought all types of records that would reveal who knew what and when.

We believed that the American public deserved to know why the Obama administration approved a deal that gave corrupt Russian nuclear powers control over so much of America's uranium production while the Clintons reaped tremendous benefit.

The agencies failed to follow the law and clear requirements of the FOIA. So we took them to federal court in Washington.

While we waited for the court to enforce the law and require the agencies to produce the records we demanded, the story continued to unfold. An FBI informant who was involved in the Uranium One deal was silenced by the Obama administration and threatened with prosecution for sharing details about it. He had given a ten-page statement to the Senate Judiciary Committee, the House Intelligence Committee, and the House Committee on Oversight and Reform, asserting that Russia had hired APCO Worldwide—a global public affairs consulting firm headquartered in Washington—to influence the Obama administration and Hillary Clinton.

According to the informant, Russian nuclear officials "told [him] at various times that they expected APCO to apply a portion of its funds received from Russia to provide in-kind support for the Clintons' Global Initiative."[30] Specifically, in exchange for Russia's payment of more than $3 million, "APCO was expected to give assistance free of charge to the Clinton Global Initiative as part of their effort to create a favorable environment to ensure the Obama administration made affirmative decisions on everything from Uranium One to the US-Russia Civilian Nuclear Cooperation agreement."[31]

This information demonstrates why it is so important to challenge the Deep State. Brave informants. Public advocacy and strategically targeted FOIA requests. Justice must be served and the truth must be disclosed.

THE SECRET CLINTON-LYNCH MEETING AND THE SHAM COMEY INVESTIGATION

Now, let's go back to the summer of 2016, June 27 to be exact. The presidential election campaigns were heating up. And Hillary Clinton was, supposedly, being investigated by the FBI for her use of a private homebrew email server to send, receive, and store classified State Department communications—in violation of federal law. It was against this setting that U.S. Attorney General Loretta Lynch thought it would be wise to meet secretly with former President Bill Clinton on Lynch's government airplane, on the tarmac at Sky Harbor International Airport in Phoenix, Arizona.

According to one report, "Lynch and Bill Clinton met privately in Phoenix Monday after the two realized they were on the same tarmac, an aide to the former president said.[32]

But other reports painted a different picture: "Clinton was reportedly notified that Lynch would be landing in Phoenix soon and waited in order to meet her,"[33] said one.

Either way, "the former president then walked over to the attorney general's plane to speak to Ms. Lynch and her husband."[34]

As reported by the *Hill*, "a law enforcement official familiar with the matter told CNN that Lynch's FBI security detail did not stop Clinton when he moved to initiate the extended conversation."[35] The meeting lasted around thirty minutes, and Attorney General Lynch later described the conversation as "primarily social."[36]

Lynch was then the nation's chief law enforcement officer under President Obama. At the time of the secret meeting, a United States district judge[37] and President Obama's White House[38] had acknowledged that the DOJ, via the FBI, was engaged in a "criminal investigation" of Hillary Clinton over her use and deletion of emails.

And, at the time of the meeting, the DOJ itself had described the investigation as a "law enforcement matter."[39]

And don't forget that fired FBI director James Comey testified the next year that Lynch had told him to call the investigation a "matter," and not an "investigation." And, according to his own testimony, he capitulated to her pressure.

Regardless, Comey's testimony nearly a year later made clear that Hillary Clinton was, indeed, under criminal investigation at the time of the secret meeting. In fact, he testified that the secret meeting is what prompted him to go public with the FBI's criminal investigation of Hillary Clinton—a breach of FBI protocol. Make no mistake, *everyone* involved in the secret meeting—as well as the attempted cover-up that would follow—knew that Hillary Clinton was being investigated by the FBI.

And, in addition to all of that, we learned later that the FBI interviewed Hillary Clinton just days after Lynch's secret meeting with Bill Clinton, over Independence Day weekend. According to reports by the *Hill* and many others, this interview was neither recorded nor transcribed, and Hillary Clinton was not placed under oath.[40] On July 5, 2016, just days after the interview, Comey issued a statement declining to recommend that she be indicted. We later obtained documents showing that his statement had been drafted well before the interview took place.

Much later, it was revealed that one of the FBI's participants in Hillary Clinton's "interview" was none other than Peter

Strzok, who was then the number two official in the FBI's Counterintelligence Division. We later learned that Strzok influenced the language of Comey's statement about why he believed that Hillary Clinton should not be charged with a crime. Comey's initial draft language described Hillary Clinton's actions as "grossly negligent"—which was problematic to her Deep State supporters for one simple reason—that is the precise language found in the United States Code describing the crime of mishandling classified information.

In other words, the initial language was damning and exposed the charade that Comey and Strzok's "investigation" of Hillary Clinton actually was. Strzok, a high-level Deep State official, changed the language to describe Hillary Clinton's actions as "extremely careless." Thanks to Strzok, Comey's final statement now read:

> Although we did not find clear evidence that Secretary Clinton or her colleagues intended to violate laws governing the handling of classified information, there is evidence that they were extremely careless in their handling of very sensitive, highly classified information.

It's clear that Comey's FBI investigation of Clinton was a sham.

We knew, when the statement was released, that Comey's use of "extremely careless" was an effort to get around using "grossly negligent"—the words found in the criminal statute. But they meant the same thing. The phoniness was obvious, but it worked. Strzok knew what he was doing.

Well after the fact, Strzok's Deep State activities and partisan underpinnings would be exposed. This is, after all, the same Peter Strzok who signed the document initiating the FBI's counterintelligence investigation into Russian interference with our elections and alleged collusion by the Trump campaign.[41] And it is the same Peter Strzok whose infamous text message exchanges with his mistress, Lisa Page, also an FBI lawyer, led to his removal from Special Counsel Robert Mueller's team, which had taken over Strzok's Russian collusion investigation. As we detailed earlier, these text messages also revealed the strong political biases and utter contempt for then-candidate Donald Trump that Strzok and others in FBI leadership held.

Amid the dizzying barrage of revelations concerning the sham Clinton investigation that Comey announced, and closed, a week after the secret tarmac meeting, it is easy to forget that all the information we know now was not revealed right away. We have been diligently chipping away for months. When the bombshell story of Lynch's secret meeting with Hillary Clinton's husband broke, we went to work at the ACLJ to get to the bottom of what was really going on. We prepared a series of FOIA requests and sent them to the DOJ and the FBI.

What we uncovered was a den of vipers in the federal government's top law enforcement agencies.

Here's what happened. In response to our FOIA request, the FBI initially sent us a letter stating that it had not located any records responsive to our request, and thus it was closing our request.

But the DOJ's production of its own responsive documents—after we filed a federal lawsuit—opened a floodgate of revelations, and more sunlight began to shine on the Deep State. One of those revelations was that FBI records certainly existed and that any reasonable search by the FBI would have uncovered them.

It was clear that Comey's FBI lied to us. So, in August of 2017, the ACLJ publicized what we had learned about the FBI's mischief. The story made headlines far and wide and led to significant public scrutiny of the FBI's apparent dishonesty.

The records the DOJ gave us also exposed the department's efforts to cover up the tarmac meeting. They showed that the news of the meeting immediately went straight to the top, i.e., to Lynch and her advisers and to then–FBI Director James Comey's chief of staff, James Rybicki. They also showed that, right away, the DOJ's spin team started manufacturing talking points for Lynch to use to deal with the press.

Unsurprisingly, the DOJ is fighting us in court to keep from having to provide those talking points, which has led us to appeal one of our cases to the D.C. Circuit Court of Appeals. The records also showed cooperation between the DOJ and the mainstream media to minimize the damage caused by the publicity surrounding the meeting. And they revealed the secret alias— "Elizabeth Carlisle"—that Lynch used for her official DOJ emails, including those about her secret tarmac meeting. More sunlight.

Now let's shift gears back to the FBI. After its public humiliation for being called out for its dishonesty, the FBI tucked its tail between its legs and sent the ACLJ a letter telling us it was reopening our FOIA request because, unsurprisingly, it had discovered that some records responsive to our request might exist after all. This move also made headlines. Incredibly, though, the FBI then ignored us, forcing us to file yet another federal lawsuit to force the Bureau to comply with the law. Finally, in response to our lawsuit, in December 2017, a year and a half after we initially filed our FOIA request, the FBI began producing its own set of records about the secret tarmac meeting.

Those records revealed that then-Director Comey learned of the meeting almost immediately after it happened and that DOJ and FBI officials colluded with each other in an attempt to minimize the damage. These records revealed further that the FBI officials were more concerned with identifying and punishing the law enforcement officer who had "leaked" to the media that the secret tarmac meeting was taking place than they were with the impropriety of the meeting itself.

The FBI's records revealed one more key fact: when the DOJ produced its records to the ACLJ, it failed to produce all of them! In particular, the DOJ withheld a key email under the subject line "Bill Clinton meeting?" which was dated June 28, 2016, that had been sent just minutes after the firestorm began. That email showed that senior DOJ officials informed the FBI of the DOJ's attempts to "deal with this" situation. Remember, it was the FBI that was investigating Hillary Clinton. Again, the DOJ had conveniently left that email out of records it gave the ACLJ. We uncovered it only because we kept digging.

The DOJ claimed in official court documents that a "glitch" in its "sophisticated" software had prevented it from locating that document. Yes, you read that right. The Deep State sure has a lot of glitches. Just like the State Department and the deleted Iran lie video, the DOJ blamed a glitch for hampering its ability to find records showing corruption. We're not buying it.

And that's the point of all of this. The only way to uncover the Deep State's virus of deception is to keep the pressure on—through the courts and through the media.

In the aftermath of the tarmac meeting, Lynch responded to concerns that her meeting created a conflict by saying that she, as head of the Department of Justice, would accept carte blanche whatever Comey recommended. In theory, by removing herself from the decision about whether to indict Hillary Clinton, whose husband had just been caught meeting with Lynch, she was removing the taint of that meeting. Never mind that the FBI, the DOJ's investigatory arm, only makes recommendations to the department and then the prosecutors at the department have an obligation to make the call, independent of the investigators and weighing a number of other factors.

With her solution, Lynch abdicated her obligation, and the role of the department, to make an independent decision. It is incredible that, in her eyes, this was not a problem. Days later, then–FBI Director Comey announced his recommendation of no charges. In making that recommendation, he knowingly usurped the critical role and power of the Department of Justice. This, ladies and gentlemen, is the Deep State.

Deep State agents within the FBI and the Department of Justice were the ones who investigated Hillary Clinton. They were the ones who wanted to bury the story of her husband's secret tarmac meeting with the attorney general. They were the ones who wanted to punish the person who revealed that the meeting had taken place. They were the ones who interviewed Hillary Clinton mere days after the secret meeting—her first and only interview with law enforcement. They were the ones who had already drafted a statement exonerating her before that interview even took place, and changed the language of that statement to protect her. And they were the ones who tried to hide the truth from us and the rest of the American public. They ultimately failed because nearly two hundred thousand Americans signed the ACLJ's petitions to investigate both Lynch and Comey, and we took action.

Here is the bottom line: Just like Lois Lerner at the IRS, none of the officials involved in this matter remain at the DOJ or FBI. Since we helped focus the spotlight on the corruption and kept digging until we uncovered a wide range of deceptions and lawlessness, numerous officials have resigned, been fired, or "retired." We not only exposed the den of vipers, our efforts helped purge them from our law enforcement agencies. Those former officials include Comey, McCabe, Rybicki, Bill Priestap (assistant director of the FBI's Counterintelligence Division who oversaw the Clinton investigation), Strzok, and Page. These individuals have two things in common: each of them turned up repeatedly in documents produced as part of our FOIA requests on these matters, and each of them is no longer in their position of power. They're gone. They're not in the Deep State anymore.

We've been asked numerous times on our radio show at the ACLJ what can be done about these Deep State officials, and this is the answer: expose them, and remove them from power.

These are just a few of the numerous examples of Deep State deception and lawlessness. The Deep State is real, it's active, and it won't go down without a fight. But, as we have shown, it can be defeated. But doing so will take the willingness of each and every one of you to defeat the corruption.

CHAPTER 7

EXPOSING THE DEN OF VIPERS— THE ACLJ FOIA PRACTICE

AT THE ACLJ, our Government Accountability Project has been dedicated to using the legal tools at our disposal to hold the Deep State accountable. The swamp in Washington is full of bureaucratic swamp creatures having spent decades ruling in D.C., running the government the way they want with little to no electoral accountability. But in recent years the swamp has gotten worse. Much worse. What our team has uncovered is a den of vipers.

Now we want to not only show you what we uncovered and how we used a critical tool at our disposal to help keep this out-of-control Deep State bureaucracy in check, but we want to empower you to use it as well. It is the Freedom of Information Act, or FOIA. Some of the biggest political corruption scandals in the past decade were exposed by the access to government records that this law mandates, and yet we'd be willing to bet most Americans, and even many who pay attention to the news, do not know what it is. Certainly even fewer know how to use it.

So we are going to walk through the basics and give some examples. This is not legal advice. It's just a road map. Whether to take the journey is up to you.

THE BASICS OF THE FOIA

Since 1967, when it was enacted, the FOIA has given Americans the right to access information from the executive branch agencies of the federal government. These are all the departments, centered in areas of Washington like Penn Quarter, Foggy Bottom, and L'Enfant Plaza. It's the Department of Justice, it's the Department of State, it's the Department of Agriculture, and it's every other department you could imagine (and maybe some you couldn't). In all, one hundred executive agencies are subject to the requirements of this law.[1] The federal courts and Congress are not, as the target of this law is the executive branch—the enforcement branch where the rubber meets the road in our federal government.

However, even with this seeming limitation, you are still able to get communications between Congress, political candidates, and even private parties as long as one of the recipients (or custodian of the records, in FOIA terminology) is a member of one of the covered executive branch agencies. This has led to the unearthing of some of the most important scandals we've seen.

From its very beginning, the act's purpose was to ensure citizens were informed about the way their government was working by giving them open access and transparency. Citizens need to know what their government is up to. In our view, the critical importance of this kind of citizen access is underscored by the simple reality that the mainstream media cannot be counted on to report everything accurately, or even to report on something at all. Without question, the free press is an invaluable American institution. Even as sloppy, fake, and openly biased as much of the press has become (something we'll detail later), it still plays an important role. Our point is that the FOIA lets us, American citizens and voters, get straight to the information. We don't have to be so dependent on the media. We can do it ourselves.

Perhaps no one described the spirit of the FOIA better than President Obama early in his first term:

> A democracy requires accountability, and accountability requires transparency. As Justice Louis Brandeis wrote, "sunlight is said to be the best of disinfectants." In our democracy, the Freedom of Information Act (FOIA), which encourages accountability through transparency, is the most prominent expression of a profound national commitment to ensuring an open Government. At the heart of that commitment is the idea that accountability is in the interest of the Government and the citizenry alike.
>
> The Freedom of Information Act should be administered with a clear presumption: In the face of doubt, openness prevails. The Government should not keep information confidential merely because public officials might be embarrassed by disclosure, because errors and failures might be revealed, or because of speculative or abstract fears. Nondisclosure should never be based on an effort to protect the personal interests of Government officials at the expense of those they are supposed to serve. In responding to requests under the FOIA, executive branch agencies...should act promptly and in a spirit of cooperation, recognizing that such agencies are servants of the public.
>
> All agencies should adopt a presumption in favor of disclosure, in order to renew their commitment to the principles embodied in FOIA, and to usher in a new era of open Government. The presumption of disclosure should be applied to all decisions involving FOIA.[2]

How ironic this pious aspiration proved to be, though, when reports indicated that the Obama-Biden administration was the least transparent in history.[3] Of course it was the Obama-Biden administration that was plagued with case after case of hidden servers, missing and deleted emails, BleachBit,[4] missing text messages, email aliases designed to subvert public sunlight, and a near-record number of lawsuits over the administration's refusal to comply with the FOIA.

As an aside, let this be a powerful reminder that when the government, or a particular career politician, says something is going to happen, that's a great start. But let's remember, there's always a place for healthy skepticism—and accountability. The results are what matters.

In spite of Obama's joke-worthy claims about the FOIA, what he said was correct! That *was* the whole point of the FOIA. That was how it was supposed to be administered by the agencies, and that was how the courts were supposed to apply it. There was supposed to be a "presumption of openness." It's built into the statute itself.

However, as you have seen, the Obama-Biden administration and the Deep State have sought to thwart the FOIA at every turn. What good is a law if it is not followed? The answer to this question is also found within the FOIA statute. If the government agency refuses or fails to provide the requested documents or a FOIA-compliant response within the statutory time frame, the requesting party can file a lawsuit in federal court to force the agency to follow the law.

At the ACLJ, that is something we have done time and time again, and with significant success. Every one of our FOIA lawsuits has forced the agencies involved to produce reams of information to the ACLJ.

While you can file your own FOIAs, you can also join ours.

We have numerous petitions at ACLJ.org allowing you not only to join our FOIA requests but also to have a voice in our FOIA lawsuits.

Through our FOIA practice and litigation, we've exposed significant corruption. In many cases, Deep State officials on whom we've collected volumes of information have been fired, have resigned, retired, or are otherwise no longer in positions of power. Here are a few examples of how your willingness to demand answers can be used to defeat the Deep State and hold our government accountable for its actions.

THE DEEP STATE POSTER CHILD—BROCK JOHNSON

In one of our FOIA cases, we found a person who we think exemplifies the Deep State as much as anyone. This person, as we came to find out, was *the* "favor" requested by the Clinton Foundation from Hillary Clinton's State Department. His name is Brock Johnson. And this is how we found him.

Based on some emails that our friends at Judicial Watch had obtained from the State Department, we learned that Clinton Foundation officials were seeking favors from Hillary Clinton's State Department. In one set of emails, Doug Band, a senior Clinton Foundation official, forwarded a request for "a favor" for someone who had joined former president Bill Clinton and United Nations Secretary-General Ban Ki-moon on an infamous trip to Haiti in 2009. That person's name was redacted.

In the email, Band told Huma Abedin and Cheryl Mills that it was "[i]mportant to take care of [redacted]." Of course, Abedin was Secretary of State Clinton's top aide at the State Department. Abedin responded: "Personnel has been sending him options." Well, that could mean a lot of different things, and in our view, it was important to find out what.

So we prepared a FOIA request demanding to know who this person was, and what, if any, job that person was offered. We sent the FOIA request in August of 2016; after the State Department ignored our request—and the requirements of the law—we filed a lawsuit in federal court in Washington. Only then did we get our first set of documents, but here is the irony: the State Department did not hand them over until the Obama-Biden administration's final night in power.

That's right. State Department officials initially ignored our FOIA request, and we took them to court. Only then, and less than twenty-four hours before President Obama left office, did they release these critical documents exposing collusion among President Obama's State Department, then–Secretary of State Hillary Clinton's senior staff, and the Clinton Foundation.

The documents we obtained showed that Johnson was, in fact, the "favor" for the Clinton Foundation. The documents included his employment file, and they showed that Johnson got a job—classified as "critical sensitive" at the State Department—just over two weeks after the initial email from Band was sent to then–Secretary of State Clinton's top aides—Abedin and Mills.

His job: "Special Assistant to the Special Envoy for Guantanamo Closure." The job description stated that he was to help the special envoy "in furtherance of President Obama's order to close the Guantanamo Bay detention facility."

Johnson was reportedly a former Obama campaign operative. His employment files show that he was quickly promoted to work directly under Mills, counselor and chief of staff to Hillary Clinton herself. His emails show that he regularly communicated with Mills and that he was a top aide to Hillary Clinton.

But Johnson wasn't just an aide, he was *the aide* who would later tip off Mills about a "Significant FOIA" request in 2012 that sought information about "the number of email accounts of, or associated with, Secretary Hillary Rodham Clinton, and the extent to which those email accounts are identifiable as those of or associated with Secretary Clinton."[5]

The State Department's inspector general later found that the State Department falsely stated that there were "no records responsive to your request," when in fact numerous officials knew about Hillary Clinton's private email address. To be clear, Johnson tipped off Mills about the FOIA request that would have first publicly uncovered Secretary Clinton's email scandal, and as a result of his tip-off, the State Department was able to cover it up for months. And Johnson obtained his job as a "favor" to the Clinton Foundation. This is the Deep State.

Further evidence obtained in this FOIA case became proof positive that not only was there no firewall between the Clinton Foundation and the State Department, as she had promised there would be, but "favor[s]" were proactively being sought and done—actual jobs were being offered. And not just any job—the job of helping close GITMO. In fact, Johnson was granted "interim clearance for access to classified information at the [redacted] level" less than two weeks after the "favor" email.

President Obama had given an "order to close the Guantanamo Bay detention facility," in direct violation of Congress's oversight. Then Hillary Clinton hired someone put forward by the Clinton Foundation as "a favor" to help close GITMO.

We had long suspected that this type of behavior was taking place, but it was only by engaging the FOIA tools that we were able to get proof. The bureaucracy is doing everything within its immense and uncontrollable power to push forward its own agenda, to hide the truth from the American people, to further corruption. This is precisely why our efforts to unearth the truth are so critical. We cannot hold them accountable if we do not know what they are doing.

Through our lawsuit, several months later, we learned that the State Department had 64,000 of Johnson's emails. These emails could show who else in the sprawling, Deep State bureaucracy was conspiring, undermining, or furthering a shadow government agenda within the department. So we demanded that the agency produce these records to us.

Shockingly, though, State Department bureaucrats told us that it would take them eighteen to thirty-six years to process this one person's emails and turn them over to us, as required by law. This was proving to be a case of justice delayed is justice denied. We asked the court to intervene. And we explained to the court that the State Department bureaucracy was not just being absurd, but that it was also frustrating the very purpose of the FOIA. Accountability for something done a year ago means nothing thirty-six years from now.

The court agreed, and noted at our first hearing that the people deserve to know what the government is doing. The judge made it clear that the State Department would be required to comply with the law in "months," adding, "I'm not talking about years." The court's displeasure with the State Department's arguments was visible—and, more important, *it was enforceable.*

But then it got worse. After that first hearing, the State Department revealed that, lo and behold, it had discovered an additional 32,000 Brock Johnson emails on its classified system (the logical result of him working in the unit the Obama administration had tasked with attempting to close GITMO).

So, after nine months, 96,000 responsive documents had been unearthed, but the Deep State bureaucrats had only turned over

145 of those documents to us. And, multiplying the absurdity, they wanted possibly thirty-six years or more to hand them all over. And they made the argument with a straight face.

At the next hearing, the court described the State Department's conduct—its slow-rolling production, delays, and refusal to comply with the basic tenets of the law—as "troubling." The court went on to order the largest court-ordered FOIA production of documents from the State Department since the 2016 election, and—as of summer 2019—we were still receiving and reviewing monthly productions of documents.

We went to court, and now we're getting answers. It's the only way to defeat the corruption. We will not back down. We will demand the truth. We will hold the out-of-control bureaucracy accountable.

What is shocking is that someone as seemingly insignificant as Brock Johnson and his involvement in efforts to cover up the Clinton email scandal that led to a fake FBI and DOJ investigation of Clinton could actually be the catalyst for uncovering a den of vipers corrupting our nation's top law enforcement agencies.

COMEY'S CIRCLE OF CORRUPTION

Fired FBI director James Comey's indiscretions, bad acts, false statements to Congress, leaks, and examples of politically motivated behavior at the FBI are almost too numerous to list. But Comey did not act alone. He had a team—an inner circle of top advisers and aides, all part of the den of vipers—who helped him drive the FBI leadership's reputation into the ground.

One key person on his team was James Baker, former general counsel for the FBI. Baker resigned from the Bureau the same day that Lisa Page, former special counsel to disgraced FBI deputy director Andrew McCabe, resigned.[6]

Almost comically, Comey said this of Baker following Baker's resignation:

> "Jim Baker represents the best of the Department of Justice and the FBI. He has protected the country and the rule of law throughout his career and leaves an inspiring legacy of service. He is what we should all hope our kids become, a person of integrity."[7]

According to reports, this person whom Comey praised so gushingly is under an active criminal investigation. As reported by Fox News chief intelligence correspondent Catherine Herridge in January 2019, "The former top lawyer at the FBI has been under federal investigation for leaking to the media, a letter from House Republicans revealed Tuesday."[8] According to the letter,

> "You may or may not know, [Baker has] been the subject of a leak investigation... a criminal leak investigation that's still active at the Justice Department," lawyer Daniel Levin told lawmakers, as he pushed back on questions about his client's conversations with reporters.[9] .

Congressmen "Jordan and Meadows' letter was sent to Durham, the U.S. attorney for Connecticut, and requested additional information about the probe later this month."[10] "A source familiar with the U.S. Attorney investigation told Fox News they believe the investigation of Baker remains open, adding they understand it began during the Obama administration and not in the course of the Russia investigation."[11]

Who is James Baker? What was he involved in? Was he a part of the FBI's blunders and political scandals? Well, let's take a look.

We learned from a blockbuster June 2018 Department of Justice Inspector General Report called *A Review of Various Actions by the Federal Bureau of Investigation and Department of Justice in Advance of the 2016 Election*[12] that James Baker was part of Comey's "core team of senior officials," which included Deputy Director McCabe, McCabe's counsel, Lisa Page (beginning in February 2016), James Rybicki (Comey's chief of staff), Trisha Anderson (Baker's deputy general counsel), "FBI Attorney 1" (who answered to Anderson), Bill Priestap (Counterintelligence Division), and Peter Strzok.[13]

The news this circle of FBI leadership has generated is astounding. It truly is Comey's circle of corruption. What is even more disturbing is the role these bad actors played in the early days of the Russia investigation and their bias against President Trump.

For example, we learned from the OIG report that Peter Strzok (and his girlfriend Lisa Page) was part of the FBI's Russia investigation, but then joined the special counsel's Russia investigation team. McCabe was involved in the Russia investigation. "FBI Attorney 1"—who answered to Baker's deputy general counsel and thus ultimately to Baker himself[14]—went on to join the FBI's Russia investigation.[15] Through public reporting, we know that Baker's role in the Russia investigation was significant. As reported by the *Daily Caller* in October 2018:

James Baker, who served as FBI's general counsel until he resigned in May, testified to Congress on Wednesday that Michael Sussmann, a lawyer for the firm Perkins Coie, provided documents and electronic media related to Russian meddling in the election.

Perkins Coie is the firm that hired opposition research [and strategic intelligence firm] Fusion GPS to investigate Trump. The result of the contract was the infamous but un-verified Steele dossier alleging collusion between the Trump campaign and Russian government....

The meeting took place before the FBI submitted an application for its first FISA warrant against former Trump campaign adviser Carter Page. That warrant application, which was granted on Oct. 21, 2016, relied heavily on unverified allegations made in the report authored by former British spy Christopher Steele.

Steele had been hired by Fusion GPS in June 2016 to investigate Trump.[16]

Baker was so close to Comey and Comey's efforts to bring down President Trump that he was one of only three people to whom Comey sent the notes he purportedly typed up in the FBI vehicle immediately after leaving his Trump Tower meeting with President-Elect Trump on January 6, 2017.[17] These were the notes Comey told Congress he leaked to his friend so that they could be leaked to the media to help influence the appointment of a special counsel. Comey classified the notes as "SECRET" at the time, testified to intentionally leaking them to the press through an agent, and then testified that he was not a leaker.[18]

Back to Baker. He was one of only three people whom Comey first told about the White House meeting, during which he says the President asked him about the investigation into Lieutenant General Michael Flynn.[19] Comey's allegations about this constitute one of the events that the special counsel was investigating as potential obstruction of justice. According to reports:

Comey told Baker and two others—...FBI [Deputy] Director Andrew McCabe and Comey's Chief of Staff Jim Rybicki—about the meeting with Trump in private conversations. Sources told Vox that Comey spoke to the three men within two days of the Oval Office meeting.[20]

Sources told Vox that Comey spoke to Baker first, asking him for legal advice. A source adds that Baker "almost certainly made extensive notes about those deliberations" about the Oval Office meeting, according to Vox.[21]

Baker's direct role in the early stages of the Russia investigation is clear. "Baker, as the FBI's top lawyer, helped secure the Foreign Intelligence Surveillance Act (FISA) warrant on [Carter] Page, as well as three subsequent renewals."[22] In fact, "Baker was a key player in successfully obtaining multiple warrants for [Carter] Page."[23] FISA applications were an area of Baker's expertise from his early career. FISA applications were a big part of what he did. In fact, during his first tenure at the DOJ before joining the FBI as Comey's general counsel, "[i]t was Baker's job to ready FISA applications for domestic surveillance."[24]

Given such a sensitive role and the trust it entailed, any unlawful leaking by Baker uncovered by the DOJ in the reported criminal leak investigation is especially alarming and egregious. The question "who watches the watchers?" comes to mind.

More recently, Baker made news when, according to one report, he testified in a closed-door deposition that he had taken Deputy Attorney General Rod Rosenstein's comments regarding wearing a wire to secretly record President Trump "very seriously."[25]

COMEY'S SHAM CLINTON INVESTIGATION

Comey's circle of corruption first came to our attention not through the Russia investigation, but through the FBI's sham investigation of Hillary Clinton over her use of a private email server for official State Department business and classified information.

At the ACLJ, we had sent a FOIA request seeking records of Comey's investigation into Hillary Clinton's actions. Once again, we had to take the FBI to federal court to get it to follow the law. Once we got the FBI under court supervision, we began receiving records.

In those records, Baker appears in multiple emails and threads wherein Comey circulated drafts of his exoneration statement in which he usurped the attorney general's authority by announcing charges would not be brought against Hillary Clinton.[26] The earliest emails here were sent by Comey to McCabe, Baker, and James Rybicki (then Comey's chief of staff), and contain significant redactions. These redactions include the names of two FBI Office of General Counsel officials. One cannot help but wonder if these two could be the infamous "FBI Attorney 1" and "FBI Attorney 2" from the Department of Justice's Office of the Inspector General report—later outed as Kevin Clinesmith and Sally Moyer.[27]

But even with the redactions, these documents show that Baker, along with Comey, McCabe, and Rybicki, truly were in the middle of what some would argue was the FBI's biggest bungle under Comey—the so-called investigation into Hillary Clinton.

These emails of draft exonerations were circulating as far back as May 2016, way before as many as seventeen witnesses—including Hillary Clinton herself—had even been interviewed by the FBI.

As we said at the ACLJ: "On July 5, 2016, James Comey, then-Director of the FBI announced during a press conference that the FBI would not be pursuing criminal charges against Secretary Clinton for the handling, or mishandling, of classified information despite the fact that 'evidence of potential violations of the statutes regarding [Secretary Clinton's] handling of classified information' existed."[28] As we pointed out, "An investigation finds the facts and then comes to a conclusion. Comey made his determination, then collected the facts. That is not how criminal investigations work. The reality is there was not an actual investigation.... Worse yet, Comey used his position of power to toy with the democratic process during a crucial election."[29]

This would all be proven true through Comey's congressional testimony, information uncovered by Congress, information uncovered by the DOJ's inspector general, and information we obtained at the ACLJ through FOIA lawsuits. We would also learn just how involved people in Comey's circle of corruption, people like James Baker, actually were.

We also found that Baker's name appears in multiple emails and threads regarding Comey's drafts of his notorious October 2016 letter to Congress announcing—just weeks before the election—that he was reopening the Clinton investigation. The documents we obtained contain redacted emails directly between Comey and Baker under the subject line, "Here is what I have drafted,"[30] and other emails showing that Baker edited Comey's draft letter.[31] And James Baker appears in an email thread we obtained concerning Comey's letter dated November 6, 2016—just two days before the election—announcing that the Clinton investigation was being closed yet again.[32]

Baker was in the middle of all of that. He was in the middle of the politicization of the FBI. He was Comey's right hand while Comey used the power of his office to manipulate the 2016 presidential election. The full story of Comey's circle of corruption at the FBI cannot be told with a single discovery or release. Congress played a role, the media played a role, and ACLJ FOIAs and multimedia platforms played a role. We get the information, study it, then share it with you. The bits and pieces trickle out one by one over time. We will continue our work to expose the truth, using information from any legitimate source we can find. And that certainly includes information we obtain by filing FOIA requests.

GOVERNMENT CORRUPTION AND HUMAN NATURE

We've established by now that corruption and government go hand in hand. And while some of the things we've discovered have shocked us, the underlying premise shouldn't really be that surprising—corruption is human nature. Our government is composed of men and women. They're human. Just like us. That fact excuses nothing. But it is important to understand nonetheless. We must have a clear-eyed vision as we view our government. There's no more time for naivete. We must be vigilant. And, like our political opponents and corrupt government actors, we must be persistent.

And one thing we've learned is that there is the underlying bad act, and then there is the act that almost always follows, the cover-up. Again, human nature. The story of man from the very beginning in the Garden of Eden. Regardless, the Deep State can cover its tracks better than anyone. It is, after all, part of the federal government, complete with all the brute force and power we the people have surrendered to it over the past 243 or so years.

And even at the state and local government levels, they still possess the power of duly vested government. The power of coercion. The power of the badge and gun. The power to prosecute. The power to take custody of children. The power to tax. The power to shut your business down. These are tremendously enormous and impactful powers. So while much of our focus tends to center on the federal government, that's mainly because that's the arena we find ourselves fighting in the most. But our message to you here is that the arenas of state, county, and city government are every bit as critical. Corruption happens everywhere humans possess power. Fortunately, many—if not most—states and municipal governments have some type of "sunshine" laws—state and local versions of the FOIA.

But here's the bottom line: The corruption is not going to disappear. So neither must our efforts to confront it.

The Deep State is relentless, and it is willing to stop at nothing. One of the best examples of this comes from one of our FOIA cases. During court-ordered negotiations, several of us found ourselves face-to-face with senior DOJ officials whose client, the agency we had sued, wanted years to produce the records we requested.

As we sat across the table from these officials attempting—at least on our part—to engage in good-faith negotiations, one Deep State actor told us point-blank that their client would refuse to budge because, even if we could persuade the judge to order faster document production, the agency would refuse to comply; it was willing to be held in contempt.

Shocked at this blatant admission, one of us looked up and responded, "We're supposed to be in good-faith negotiations." The law was clear, but they were willing to flout it, even to the point of being held in contempt of court. Though we pushed back aggressively, the negotiations didn't get us anywhere. But in the end, we obtained a court order, and succeeded in getting key documents.

The incident shows that the Deep State is real. And to defeat it, you have to stand up and fight back.

The FOIA is a remarkable asset in our struggle. You don't have to be lawyers to use it. Any American can submit a FOIA request. While you can find our FOIA requests on our website at ACLJ.org to use as samples, you can also join our FOIAs and our lawsuits. We are providing you with the opportunity to use these tools with us to make a significant impact. These are just a few examples of the corruption we've uncovered and the success we've had.

Comey's circle of corruption is now almost completely out of business. He, McCabe, and Strzok were fired; Baker and Rybicki resigned or otherwise left the FBI. Like Lerner at the IRS, these Deep State officials are gone from the government. And even now this den of vipers is turning on each other. That's a victory— a victory you helped make possible.

But this is not the time to rest. It's time to get to work.

CHAPTER 8

YOUR VOICE—GLOBAL IMPACT

MAKING AN IMPACT at home is important, but the next red wave
will be about more than domestic elections. What about a global
impact? Can you—one person—really have an impact on the
global problems we face?

It's easy to see how you can have an impact at home. As a
citizen of America, you have the right to vote. Everyone knows
that. But, internationally, you are just one of more than 7.7 billion people. And the problems we are facing on the world stage
are big. Unfathomably big.

When you think about the next red wave, global impact may
not come to mind. But it should.

Just consider the problem of the jihadist genocide that the Islamic State—ISIS—has been committing against Christians in
the Middle East (something we will discuss in depth in the next
chapter). For years, you've heard about the barbarity that was
perpetrated against innocent civilians. It makes you feel almost
helpless.

What about Christians who have been thrown in jail or who
are even on death row in repressive regimes—merely because of
their faith?

In the face of so much evil, you want to act, but what can you do? When hundreds of girls were kidnapped by Boko Haram— a radical Islamist group that has pledged allegiance to ISIS in Nigeria—people wanted to act. They started a hashtag campaign on Twitter—#BringBackOurGirls. Unfortunately, what started out based on a pure desire to help became a celebrity piggyback campaign. The Obama administration, which was then in office, could have taken action, creating an international coalition to rescue the girls. Instead, Michelle Obama posted an image of herself on social media holding a piece of paper that read, "#Bring-BackOurGirls."

Social campaigns can be great, but they must lead to concrete action if they are going to be effective. A hashtag for the sake of a hashtag is just a hashtag. A hashtag never saved anyone. So while the Left, the Obama administration, and the media were fixated on a hashtag, nothing changed for these poor defenseless girls for months on end.[1] In fact, Boko Haram has been emboldened, employing the same kidnapping tactic again and again.

So what can you do? Are you relegated to hashtag advocacy? Is hashtag diplomacy our only avenue to effect global change? NO! Of course not.

As we will explain, social media and social advocacy can be powerful tools, but you have to tie them to concrete steps.

You can do it. You can be the voice for the voiceless. You can defend persecuted Christians halfway around the world. What we're about to share with you isn't revolutionary. It is tried-and-true. And it is incredibly effective.

A core aspect of our mission at the ACLJ is defending persecuted Christians across the globe. We've secured the release of persecuted pastors in Iran, Sudan, and Turkey. We've rescued Christians from Palestinian persecution, Iranian death sentences, and Pakistani hangings. We operate offices in Jerusalem, Africa, Pakistan, and other persecution hot spots.

In most cases, we don't have attorneys on the ground in places like Iran and Sudan—if we were to set foot in any of those countries, we would likely be thrown into prison ourselves, never to be heard from again. But we are able to effectively utilize the voices of thousands of people across the globe to save lives. We call it legal advocacy. We employ action to get results. You can be a part of this.

"REMEMBER THE PRISONERS, AS THOUGH IN PRISON WITH THEM"

Hebrews 13:3 says, "Remember the prisoners, as though in prison with them, and those who are ill-treated, since you yourselves also are in the body."[2] At the ACLJ, we take this seriously. It's the starting point of our global legal advocacy.

Christians suffering in prisons across the globe because of their faith need an advocate. They need someone—lots of someones—willing to be their voice. The faceless persecuted must be given a face. They are suffering humans. We don't look at any of them as a number, as one of thousands imprisoned for their faith.

We take one case at a time. We've implemented a multipronged legal advocacy strategy that focuses on an individual facing immense persecution. Thankfully, we have been blessed with great success.

We amplify. We advocate. And we aggressively apply pressure. Here in the United States, with world leaders, and in the persecuting country. This method has led to the freedom of nearly a dozen high-profile individuals from some of the worst situations imaginable in just the last few years—a near-perfect success rate.

Here are two of those stories:

American Pastor Andrew Brunson, fifty-one, ministered to the people of Turkey without issue for more than twenty-three years. While he and his family are U.S. citizens from North Carolina, he pastored a local church in Turkey, where he had no run-ins with the government.

Then, shortly after surviving a failed coup attempt in July 2016, Turkey's president, Recep Tayyip Erdoğan, issued an emergency declaration expanding his powers. He used the coup attempt as a pretense to round up political enemies and religious minorities to gain political and diplomatic leverage.

Pastor Brunson was picked up as part of this crackdown on October 7, 2016. He was falsely charged with membership in an armed terrorist organization and other charges related to national security. Around the world, time and again, we have seen that "national security" has become cover for imprisoning and persecuting Christians. After more than a year, the Turkish government finally released official charging documents, which charged Pastor Brunson with "Christianization."[3] They actually came right out and said it.

Shortly after his arrest, Pastor Brunson's wife contacted us. We at the ACLJ began representing the family. We launched a massive legal and media global advocacy campaign. We went to Congress, we went to the White House, we went to the State Department, we went to the United Nations, and we engaged with Turkish officials. We utilized social media to share the pastor's story. We engaged with traditional media to raise awareness of his plight.

But what we did couldn't possibly have had the power and effectiveness that it did have without you. The first thing we did was launch a petition for Pastor Brunson's freedom. In the end, nearly six hundred thousand people signed that petition. Individuals from all over the world showed that they cared about what happened to this one pastor in Turkey.

It got Turkey's attention. It also got the attention of world leaders and our own government.

This example also shows what a difference an election can make. As soon as Trump was elected president, we noticed an immediate and marked difference in the way his administration responded to these cases versus the way the Obama administration had.

For example, it took years of congressional testimony, constant media saturation, and flat-out embarrassing the Obama administration to get President Obama to engage in a similar case in Iran. For three years, a U.S. citizen sat in a horrendous prison in Iran simply because he was a Christian, and the Obama administration wouldn't lift a finger. We eventually secured his freedom, too, but it was a lot harder. That also makes an important point: even in the most unfriendly of political environments, you *still* can have a massive impact when you are willing to stand up and be heard.

When hundreds of thousands of people signed our petitions, wrote letters, and joined our advocacy efforts, it became impossible for even the Obama administration to ignore us. Which brings us to an important point. Part of bringing about the next red wave is making yourself impossible to ignore. It's like the parable of the persistent widow. In Luke 18, Jesus told the story:

> Then Jesus told his disciples a parable to show them that they should always pray and not give up. He said: "In a certain town there was a judge who neither feared God nor cared what people thought. And there was a widow in that town who kept coming to him with the plea, 'Grant me justice against my adversary.'

"For some time he refused. But finally he said to himself, 'Even though I don't fear God or care what people think, yet because this widow keeps bothering me, I will see that she gets justice, so that she won't eventually come and attack me!'"

And the Lord said, "Listen to what the unjust judge says. And will not God bring about justice for his chosen ones, who cry out to him day and night? Will he keep putting them off? I tell you, he will see that they get justice, and quickly. However, when the Son of Man comes, will he find faith on the earth?"[4]

Don't stop knocking. Don't stop petitioning. Don't stop exercising your free speech. Eventually, they won't be able to ignore you anymore.

So even when those whom you don't support and who don't care about what you think are in power, it's critical to never give up. You can still make an impact.

But it certainly is a lot more effective when the right people are in office. In the case of Pastor Brunson, we noticed an immediate change. President Trump actually cared. He cared about a U.S. citizen imprisoned in a faraway land. He cared about Pastor Brunson. He took to his biggest megaphone and tweeted, putting the world on notice that he was working to secure Pastor Brunson's freedom.

And he was relentless. President Trump imposed sanctions on Turkey. He raised Pastor Brunson's case every time he talked with Turkey's president. He did not give up until Pastor Brunson was free. Neither did key members of his administration.

Your vote put President Trump in office. And your voice helped give us the tools we needed to secure Pastor Brunson's freedom.

As a result of your efforts, your voice was having a tremendous influence in the halls of power. After about two years of written legal submissions and oral interventions at the U.N. Human Rights Council, tireless advocacy on Capitol Hill, and relentless work with the Trump administration to pressure Turkey, we were able to secure the release of Pastor Brunson, who was allowed to return home to his family in America.

It was a tremendous victory; won because individuals were willing to speak out.

This was a U.S. citizen, so we focused our advocacy efforts here in the United States and in the persecuting nation, Turkey.

But the tactic is different when the person being persecuted is a citizen of the country that is doing the persecuting. This was the case with Asia Bibi. In 2009, this Christian mother of five was picking berries in the fields of Pakistan. She selflessly and lovingly offered one of her coworkers—a Muslim coworker—a sip of water. The coworker declined, claiming that the water was now unclean because Asia Bibi was a Christian. A disagreement arose, and in the end the Muslim coworker and a nearby Muslim cleric falsely accused Asia Bibi of blasphemy—speaking against the Prophet Muhammad.

All too often, we see in Muslim-majority nations false blasphemy accusations being used to punish religious minorities. This is what happened to Asia Bibi. She was run roughshod through a faulty trial, convicted of blasphemy, and sentenced to execution by hanging. After years of sitting on death row, she saw the denial of her first level of appeal.

That's when we heard about the case and got involved. Unfortunately, many of these cases end horribly because no one finds out what happened until it is too late to intervene. The victims just disappear. Thankfully, we found Asia Bibi's case and went to work.

Again, we began with a petition. Over the course of more than four years of advocacy, we gathered nearly 825,000 signatures on Asia Bibi's behalf. While we did advocate here in the United States, we focused most of our work internationally. We used our offices in Pakistan and our international affiliate office with consultative status at the United Nations, the European Centre for Law and Justice (ECLJ), to place massive pressure on Pakistan.

We engaged with the media to ensure that Asia Bibi remained in the headlines and was not forgotten.

We took each one of those 825,000 voices to world leaders. We took them all to the United Nations multiple times. We showed that the world was watching.

Many times, even repressive regimes actually do care what the world thinks. They may not act like they do, but they do. They want to carry out persecution without the world ever finding out. When they are caught, they may stall and delay and hope the world loses interest, but they eventually cave.

It's the persistent widow. When individual after individual refuses to be ignored, the impact becomes exponential.

After years of advocacy that saw the resignation of a Pakistani Supreme Court justice, riots in the streets of Pakistan, and immense global pressure on Islamabad, Asia Bibi was finally released from death row in November 2018. Her execution sentence and conviction for blasphemy were overturned by the Pakistani Supreme Court. While Pakistan used the courts to acquit her, Asia Bibi can credit the international outcry for her freedom, after eight years on death row.

That outcry was strengthened by your voice and the voices of hundreds of thousands of people just like you. But your voice can be heard only if you speak. Silence in cases where Christians are being persecuted can be deafening. And it can literally be deadly.

These cases take a long time to unfold. Persistence is the key. Your voice is the tool.

YOUR VOICE MAKES A GLOBAL IMPACT

We know that when Americans are willing to speak out and *demand* action—not just lip service—we can make an impact across the globe. And that's the point. Advocacy can work. When we make a plan and act on it, persistently, we can succeed. We must understand the big picture, and keep chipping away at our goals until we accomplish them. This is how the Left has outsmarted conservatives for years. No more.

And what about that global impact? It isn't limited to cases of persecution. There are numerous examples where your voice can make a difference. One of the biggest examples may be the opening of the U.S. Embassy to Israel in Jerusalem.

For years, we have aggressively demanded—with the outspoken support of hundreds of thousands of our ACLJ members—that the U.S. government should honor U.S. law and officially recognize that Jerusalem is Israel's capital.

In 1995, Congress passed a law requiring the U.S. Embassy in Israel to move from Tel Aviv to Jerusalem. The Jerusalem Embassy Act of 1995 provides:

1. Jerusalem should remain an undivided city in which the rights of every ethnic and religious group are protected;
2. Jerusalem should be recognized as the capital of the State of Israel; and
3. the United States Embassy in Israel should be established in Jerusalem no later than May 31, 1999.[5]

Nearly twenty years after that date, the law still had not been implemented. Why? The law contained a provision allowing the President to issue a waiver delaying the move for six months. And every six months since this law was to have come into force every President—Bill Clinton, George W. Bush, and Obama—issued the waiver, delaying the move.

President Trump changed all that. In late 2017, he recognized Jerusalem as the official capital of Israel, just as he had promised during the campaign. Not only did he officially recognize Jerusalem as the capital—a historical reality supported by U.S. and international law and consistent with the facts on the ground—but he also ordered that the U.S. Embassy be moved to Jerusalem from Tel Aviv.

President Trump's official proclamation was bold and clear:

The foreign policy of the United States is grounded in principled realism, which begins with an honest acknowledgment of plain facts. With respect to the State of Israel, that requires officially recognizing Jerusalem as its capital and relocating the United States Embassy to Israel to Jerusalem as soon as practicable.

The Congress, since the Jerusalem Embassy Act of 1995 (Public Law 104-45) (the "Act"), has urged the United States to recognize Jerusalem as Israel's capital and to relocate our Embassy to Israel to that city. The United States Senate reaffirmed the Act in a unanimous vote on June 5, 2017.

Now, 22 years after the Act's passage, I have determined that it is time for the United States to officially recognize Jerusalem as the capital of Israel. This long overdue recognition of reality is in the best interests of both the United States and the pursuit of peace between Israel and the Palestinians.

Seventy years ago, the United States, under President Truman, recognized the State of Israel. Since then, the State of Israel has made its capital in Jerusalem—the capital the Jewish people established in ancient times. Today, Jerusalem is the seat of Israel's government—the home of Israel's parliament, the Knesset; its Supreme Court; the residences of its Prime Minister and President; and the headquarters of many of its government ministries. Jerusalem is where officials of the United States, including the President, meet their Israeli counterparts. It is therefore appropriate for the United States to recognize Jerusalem as Israel's capital.

I have also determined that the United States will relocate our Embassy to Israel from Tel Aviv to Jerusalem. This action is consistent with the will of the Congress, as expressed in the Act.[6]

On May 14, 2018, President Trump fulfilled that promise, opening the embassy in Jerusalem.

This is yet another example of how your impassioned voice can change the course of international events. You can have a remarkable impact when you join with others of like mind to advocate for conservative causes. You can make history.

Your voice matters. Your vote matters. Because you elected President Trump, we now see America turning back from the blatant betrayal of Israel at the United Nations that we saw during the Obama years and supporting the only true democracy in the Middle East. Since President Trump's election, the United States has withdrawn from the U.N. Human Rights Council, refusing to condone its constant badgering of Israel and unwillingness to truly defend human rights. The United States has vetoed resolutions to condemn Israel—a marked change from the Obama administration's eleventh-hour betrayal of Israel at the United Nations allowing the U.N. Security Council to condemn not the terrorists but Israel. Congress passed and President Trump signed commonsense legislation stopping U.S. tax dollars from going to the Palestinian Authority as long as it continues to pay the families of terrorists who kill Israelis and Americans through its "pay-for-slay" program.

See? Elections have global consequences.

These are just a few of the international victories that your voice—combined with your vote—has helped achieve. It's the beginning of an international red wave that we must continue.

We must not allow the gains we've made to be lost. That will require vigilance.

Politicians are fickle. No matter their promises, they can and often will let you down on the biggest issues.

But that is why we fight. That is why we mobilize. And in the face of seemingly insurmountable obstacles, it is vital that we take the time to understand *how* we can win.

The America we all want is an America willing to use its power and might to defend what is right and to protect the persecuted. Because of your willingness to speak out and act, it is doing just that.

CHAPTER 9

DEFEATING GENOCIDE

ONE OF THE BEST examples of the power of your voice to change the world is the battle to defend Christians in the Middle East from genocide.

Over recent years, we have ensured that the voices of hundreds of thousands of people, from all across the world, were heard by high-level U.S. and U.N. officials, as well as by some of the world's most powerful leaders. But we didn't just take your voice to power. We forced action.

The key to being heard isn't just to make noise. The key to being heard is funneling your passion and vision into action.

THE GENOCIDE

In the summer of 2014, we began hearing stories of a particular unmistakable evil growing in the Middle East. A radical jihadist army was forming. It wasn't a terror cell. It was a radical Islamic army. We began hearing stories of unthinkable brutality. And we began studying them. When no one else was paying much attention, we were digging to learn more about the group and its leader.

In the fall of 2014, I helped coauthor the number one *New York Times* bestselling book *Rise of ISIS: A Threat We Can't Ignore* with my dad, Jay Sekulow. Because that's what was happening. The world was ignoring this growing jihadist army.

We began telling the stories of atrocities. We forced the world to look at the utter evil that was growing in Iraq and Syria. But we didn't stop there. In August of 2014, we launched a petition at ACLJ.org highlighting what was becoming a genocide of Christians. And, by the end of that month, we had sent our first submission to the U.N. Human Rights Council, through our international affiliate, the European Centre for Law and Justice (ECLJ), which has consultative status as a nongovernmental organization at the United Nations.

Here's what we discovered was happening in Iraq and Syria:

ISIS's systematic pattern of widespread sexual abuse and murder was forcing thousands of Christians and other religious minorities to flee from Iraq and Syria. These acts were leading to the wholesale destruction of Christians in the region. A growing body of evidence demonstrated that the inhuman violence was, in fact, genocide as defined by U.S. law[1] and the Convention on the Prevention and Punishment of the Crime of Genocide[2]—a genocide targeting Christians.

In the summer of 2014, ISIS leader Abu Bakr al-Baghdadi, as self-proclaimed Caliph Ibrahim, declared the creation of an Islamic caliphate under his leadership. ISIS then began systematically killing Christians, Yazidis (another religious and ethnic minority), and other non-Muslim and Muslim minorities who did not adhere to ISIS's sadistic ideology. ISIS members killed Christians and Yazidis by the thousands, enslaved and raped thousands more because of their religion, and destroyed their places of worship, their homes, and their livelihoods.[3]

In Iraq and Syria, Christians represent a small minority of the population, making up roughly 8 percent of the Syrian population[4] and less than 3 percent of the Iraqi population.[5]

The Christian population in both Syria and Iraq has been decimated. In fact, hundreds of thousands of Christians have fled Syria and Iraq since the rise of the Islamic State.[6] The Islamic State's barbarity knows no bounds.

In Syria, the Islamic State has beheaded and stoned men, women, and children for blasphemy, heresy, and apostasy.[7] One Christian Syrian woman described " 'Christians being killed and tortured, and . . . children being beheaded in front of their parents.' "[8] She spoke of "250 children [who] were put in the dough mixer, they were kneaded. The oldest one of them was four-years-old."[9] At times, the Islamic State also demanded that religious minorities pay a tax (called *jizya*), or flee—punishing by death those who failed to comply.[10]

In Iraq, the Islamic State's religion-targeted abuses included beheadings, burning victims alive in caskets, and other "killings, rape, kidnapping, enslavement, theft . . . destruction of religious sites . . . sexual slavery, forced conversion, ransom demands, property seizures, and forced business closures."[11]

Virtually every day, we saw new reports and accounts of the Islamic State's barbarism. Any question as to the genocidal nature of the atrocities committed against Christians and other religious and ethnic minorities had been answered in the affirmative.

Yet the world was virtually silent. Hundreds of thousands of people cared deeply. They wanted to act, but they didn't know how they could make a difference.

As we launched our petition, they began to find out how. Hundreds of thousands of people wanted action. And act we did. At the ACLJ, we began sending legal letters to U.S. government officials—then-President Obama and then–Secretary of

State John Kerry—to world leaders, to U.N. officials, and to the U.N. Human Rights Council.

THE GENOCIDE CAMPAIGN

To date, we've sent over one hundred individual legal letters to officials in more than sixty-four countries, and submitted numerous documents and oral presentations to the U.N. Human Rights Council.

We have detailed what we have been able to learn about the ongoing atrocities, reporting information that was getting scant coverage in the mainstream media—much of this information coming from firsthand accounts of the genocide on the ground.

In the ACLJ's legal letters to the United Nations and to world leaders, we detailed what we had learned about horrific abuses in Iraq. For instance, here is what we said in one of our letters[12] to the then-president of the U.N. Security Council:

The Islamic State's notorious abuses are targeted primarily against religious minorities, including an estimated 200,000 Iraqi Christians in 2014. In June 2014, after the Islamic State seized the city of Mosul, Iraq, it demanded that Christian residents either convert to Islam, pay a tax for protection, or be executed; further, the Islamic State gave the Christians less than a week (14 to 19 July) to make their decision. Several important religious sites and Christian institutions in Mosul were destroyed.

Islamic State fighters destroyed Iraq's oldest Christian monastery, St. Elijah's. Father Paul Thabit Habib, a Catholic priest "who now lives in Kurdish-administered Irbil," said that Iraq's "Christian history was 'being barbarically leveled.'" He added, "'We see it as an attempt to expel us from Iraq, eliminating and finishing our existence in this land.'" Such savagery has been punctuated by evidence that the Islamic State is burning Christians alive in locked caskets.

In June 2014, an Iraqi Christian mother and her daughter were brutally raped by Islamic State members "in front of the husband and father. The husband and father was so traumatized that he committed suicide." Four other Iraqi Christian women were shot to death by members of the Islamic State for not wearing veils.

In May 2016, Islamic State members in Mosul, Iraq, burned a twelve-year-old Christian girl to death: The "jihadi fighters had come to claim a religious tax from the girl's mother…but when the mother delayed in paying," they set fire to the family home while the mother and her daughter were still inside. The "mother and child were able to escape the burning building, but the girl had suffered such severe burns that she later died in the hospital."

And consider the story of this man, who specifically mentioned a United Nations' visit to his region:

"On 7/27/2014 during the visit to the area by the officials in the Iraqi government, led by the Speaker of Parliament we presented them with what happened to us and asked for their help to no avail. **We did the same during the UN visit to the area again to no avail. I feel we are neglected in the refugee camps and no one cares about us like we are not human.**"[13]

We highlighted the grotesque atrocities being carried out in Syria:

In Syria, the Islamic State has beheaded and stoned men, women, and children for blasphemy, heresy, and apostasy….

"In Syria...the organization Aid to the Church in Need has reported on mass graves of Christians" found in Sadad, Syria, after an "Islamist rebel siege" left as many as 45 dead, 30 wounded, and 10 missing. "Melkite Catholic Archbishop Jean-Clément Jeanbart of Aleppo estimates the number of Christians kidnapped and/or killed in his city as [being] in the hundreds, with as many as 'thousands' killed throughout Syria."...

In fact, according to other reports, the Islamic State's ultimatums to Christians living in Raqqa City, Syria, in February 2014, resulted in nearly all of the Christians fleeing their homes. The property of the Christians who fled was confiscated, and all churches in the city were transformed into mosques. Remaining residents were forbidden from worshipping according to any religion other than Islam. According to eye-witnesses who were present in the city, very few Christians remained after the Islamic State issued its ultimatum, and those who chose to remain and pay jizya were forced to pay the Islamic State a tax totaling $335 per family per year.

In February 2015, the Islamic State took approximately 230 Assyrian Christians hostage "after overrunning several communities on the southern bank of the Khabur River in northeastern Hassakeh province" in Syria. During the attacks, thousands fled. One year later, the last of the living hostages were released after the Islamic State "receiv[ed] millions of dollars in ransom." The fate of at least five of the hostages is unknown. According to other reports, between 9 and 15 Christians were killed, and 373 were taken hostage.

In August 2015, twelve Syrian Christians (including men, women, and children) were brutally and publicly tortured and executed in a village near Aleppo, Syria, because they refused to convert to Islam. Islamic State members cut off a young boy's fingertips and beat him as they demanded that his father and two other men renounce Christianity, before executing all four by crucifixion. Eight women were also publicly raped and beheaded after they refused to renounce Christianity.

In December 2015, reports surfaced that the Islamic State was responsible for multiple bombings in Kamishli, Syria, that targeted Assyrian and Kurdish Christians and killed nineteen.[14]

Forcing world leaders to face the ghastly reality of what was happening in the Middle East not only served as a wakeup call to many, but also allowed us to present clear and convincing evidence that genocide was, in fact, happening.

We also explained how ISIS's horrific brutality was spreading across the globe:

In February 2015, the Islamic State "released a video of 21 Coptic Christians from Egypt being executed on a Libyan beach." And, in April 2015, it executed at least 30 Ethiopian Christians in Libya. "One group is beheaded on a beach along the Mediterranean Sea, while the other group is shot in Southern Libya."

In June 2016, "eight suicide bombers launched two waves of attacks on the Christian town of Al Qaa in northeastern Lebanon." The New York Times reported that "four attackers blew themselves up in the town before dawn, killing five people and wounding a dozen others, according to local officials. Four more attacks took place at night as residents prepared for funerals to be held [that week], wounding 11 more people." "'People are stuck in their houses, not daring to go out and fearing more suicide bombers,' the Rev. Elian Nasrallah, the priest of the town's Mar Elias Church," told reporters. "He had been in his home at night, preparing his message for the funerals of those killed that morning, when he heard an explosion and saw a ball of fire erupt outside the church. 'We're living in terror in this town,' he said." According to reports, "nearly all experts believe it was carried out by ISIS fighters who infiltrated al-Qaa from nearby Syria." *"Make no mistake, the[y] targeted [the] village for one reason: it is Christian."*

In July 2016, Islamic State "soldiers" slit the throat of an eighty-five-year-old Catholic priest in a church near Normandy, France, during Mass. Reuters reported that according to the Islamic State's news agency, Amaq, the Islamic State claimed the two attackers as its "soldiers." According to French officials, "one of the two suspects in the attack was known to anti-terror authorities after attempting a trip to Syria." The spread of Islamic State genocide against Christians—and its direct link to Syria—should come as no surprise: "For two years, the black-clad jihadist army has called for attacks on Christians in Rome, throughout Europe and across the world. It has even called for the assassination of Pope Francis."

In February 2017, ISIS released a video making reference to its December 2016 bombing of a Christian church in Egypt, and described Christians as its "favorite prey." Just weeks later, ISIS claimed responsibility for the bombing of two churches on Palm Sunday in Egypt that killed 49 and injured more than one hundred people. The Islamic State also claimed responsibility for the failed attack on Saint Catherine's Monastery in Sinai. While the attack failed, the Islamic State "has vowed more attacks against Christians in Egypt."

In December 2017, the Islamic State claimed responsibility for an attack on a Methodist church in southwestern Pakistan, "during a Sunday pre-Christmas service," where "at least nine worshipers were killed and over 50 others were injured."[15]

Then we detailed under international law how this overwhelming body of evidence led to one unmistakable conclusion: ISIS was waging genocide against Christians and other religious minorities and the international community had a legal obligation to act. We reminded numerous international government leaders that:

As recognised in the [Genocide] Convention,
"genocide means any of the following acts committed with intent to destroy, in whole or in part, a national, ethnical, racial or religious group, as such:
(a) Killing members of the group;
(b) Causing serious bodily or mental harm to members of the group;
(c) Deliberately inflicting on the group conditions of life calculated to bring about its physical destruction in whole or in part;
(d) Imposing measures intended to prevent births within the group;
(e) Forcibly transferring children of the group to another group."
Such provisions mean little if the United Nations fails to recognise particular acts as acts of genocide.
The growing body of evidence demonstrates that the inhuman violence at issue is, in fact, genocide as defined by the Convention. . . .

Reliance on jizya to deny genocide also fails under international law. Forcible conversion coupled with destruction of Christian places of worship are acts that by their very nature are intended to destroy Christians as a religious group. Destruction of places of worship is generally "designed to annihilate the centuries-long presence of the group." If Christians succumb to forced conversion, there will be no such group called Christians in Iraq and Syria. If they do not convert and refuse (or are unable) to pay jizya, they will be killed. Either way, Christians as a religious group will cease to exist in the region—a clearly stated and demonstrated goal of the Islamic State. Moreover, just because the Islamic State *may* allow *some* Christians to pay jizya to spare their lives does not negate Islamic State actors' intent to destroy Christians as a religious group. The fact that some Christians have not been killed does not legitimise the many instances where thousands have been killed.

Furthermore, international law does not require that the targeted group be destroyed completely in order for it to constitute genocide. Intending to destroy the targeted group "*in part*" fully suffices. As such, one cannot legitimately claim that, because *some* Christians can, allegedly, save their lives by paying jizya, the Islamic State is not engaged in the genocide of Christians....

Once the United Nations as an organisation recognises the genocide as such, *then* it may properly mobilise the international community to honour the terms of the Genocide Convention and fulfill its responsibility to protect....

According to the Genocide Convention, "[t]he Contracting Parties confirm that genocide...is a crime under international law which they undertake to prevent and punish." The Convention makes clear that "the competent organs of the

United Nations" have a responsibility "to take such action under the Charter of the United Nations as they consider appropriate for the prevention and suppression of acts of genocide." According to the Office of the Special Adviser on the Prevention of Genocide, "the duty to prevent and halt genocide and mass atrocities lies first and foremost with the State, but the international community has a role." . . .

It is *this* responsibility and obligation that we urge the Security Council to advance forthwith by first recognising the ongoing atrocities as genocide, then by mobilising along with other appropriate organs of the United Nations to take action.[16]

More than just presenting the evidence of genocide and providing the legal analysis, we took the voice of the American people directly to these world leaders. We also took your voice directly to the White House and the U.S. secretary of state. And this is what began to make the difference.

What happened next was miraculous; it also shows that your voice can have an impact no matter whom you are trying to force into action.

FORCING THE OBAMA ADMINISTRATION TO ACT

Even with the evidence, the law on our side, and the voices of more than 450,000 people, the stiffest opposition we faced at the time came from the Obama administration. Our "ask" was basic and simple, yet profound. We were asking the administration to recognize the indisputable facts on the ground and call the unthinkable atrocities being inflicted on Christians what they were—genocide.

But the Obama administration knew that officially labeling the atrocities as genocide would trigger specific legal obligations: It would require the U.S. government to take steps to stop the genocide; it would require the U.S. government to garner an international coalition to defeat ISIS; and it would force the U.S. government to provide certain, basic legal protections for Christians and other religious minorities threatened with genocide on the international stage.

But this went directly against the Obama administration's narrative. The narrative that ignored the true impact of jihad. The narrative that ISIS was the "JV squad."

Simply put, to acknowledge the genocide would have required a complete retooling of the Obama administration's agenda and policy with regard to radical Islam. It was a red line that the administration refused to cross.

In fact, and perhaps even worse, when the administration began considering a recognition that ISIS had been committing genocide, it considered recognizing only the genocide against Yazidis and specifically leaving Christians off of the list of victims. The administration could then point to the one action it had taken—rescuing and providing some aid for Yazidis on top of Mount Sinjar when ISIS had encircled the refuge and was attempting to starve this minority group into extinction—as fulfilling its requirements under international law. In other words, the administration was going to recognize the genocide and, at the same time, point to a past action to satisfy its legal obligations—an attempt to get the American people off its back and give them a false sense of justice.

We would have none of it. The nearly half million people who signed our petition to recognize the genocide and protect Christians were infuriated. We went on to wage a massive legal and media advocacy campaign—again taking the voices of those who had signed our petition to both then–Secretary of State John Kerry and the rest of the Obama administration.

After years of tireless effort, we succeeded in embarrassing the Obama administration into taking action.

Sometimes you have to do that. Sometimes you have to force political leaders to do the right thing. You have to be consistent and you have to be relentless.

You see, it doesn't matter whether they are Republicans or Democrats—President Obama or President Trump. You can effectuate change. And it doesn't always have to be through the court systems. It can be (and in fact the courts played a role in this case, too). But you can also effectively advocate for change in the court of public opinion. That is sometimes the most effective forum for catalyzing cultural, moral, policy, and yes, even legal change.

And we did just that. After listening to our unyielding advocacy—and the voices of nearly half a million people—on March 17, 2016, John Kerry declared that ISIS was "responsible for genocide against groups in areas under its control, including Yazidis, Christians and Shiite Muslims."[17] It was a monumental change in official U.S. policy. And it has remained U.S. policy. President Trump's then–secretary of state, Rex Tillerson, reaffirmed this position in August 2017, stating that "ISIS is clearly responsible for genocide against Yazidis, Christians and Shia Muslims."[18]

The U.S. recognition of genocide was critical, but it was just the first step. We had to build on that momentum. These could not be just words. We had to force action.

THE SEVEN-POINT PLAN

On April 22, 2016, we at the ACLJ called for the implementation of a seven-point plan[19] to end the genocide against Christians and other religious minorities, aid the victims, and bring the perpetrators to justice.

The plan was simple, powerful, and straightforward. As we detailed it at the time:

First, call upon the United Nations (U.N.) Secretary General and the High Commissioner for Human Rights to formally recognize the genocide against Christians and demand that the U.N. as a whole do so as well—as have the U.S. Department of State, the U.S. House of Representatives, the U.S. Commission on International Religious Freedom, the Holy See's representative at the U.N. in Geneva and Pope Francis, the Parliamentary Assembly of the Council of Europe, and the European Parliament.

The U.N. High Commissioner for Human Rights has acknowledged the international community's duty to act stating, "To take one utterly shameful example, despite the horrific human rights violations in Syria that have been investigated, enumerated, discussed, we must continue to deplore the international community's failure to act."

The U.N. Secretary General has already recognized the international community's "responsibility to use appropriate diplomatic, humanitarian and other peaceful means, in accordance with Chapters VI and VIII of the Charter, to help to protect populations from genocide." So has the U.N. General Assembly. The U.N. must now recognize the ongoing ISIS atrocities as genocide against Christians and other religious minorities and act....

Second, call upon the U.N. Office of Special Adviser on the Prevention of Genocide to fulfill its role "as a catalyst...to alert relevant actors where there is a risk of genocide, and to advocate and mobilize for appropriate action"— "appropriate action" being any action that stops this genocide.

Third, call upon the U.N. Security Council to refer the matter of genocide prosecution to the International Criminal Court; or establish "ad hoc tribunals" for genocide prosecution as was done in response to the horrific genocides in Rwanda and Yugoslavia. These mechanisms are appropriate under the circumstances and based on international law and precedent. We will also urge the U.N. Security Council to consider all options available to it (including resolutions, military, and peacekeeping initiatives) to stop the genocide and protect Christians.

Fourth, demand international intervention, by any means necessary, to protect Christians and other religious minorities from genocide. International law requires that when a State (such as Syria and Iraq) "is manifestly failing to protect its populations" from genocide—as the countries overrun by ISIS's jihadist army are clearly incapable of stopping the genocide against Christians—"the international community must be prepared to take collective action to protect populations." We must assist in making the case that the contracting states involved here, Iraq and Syria, are incapable of prosecuting genocide and protecting Christians from genocide— thus activating the international community's duty to act.

Fifth, call upon the President, the U.S. Department of State, and the U.S. delegation to the U.N. to demand U.N. action as set forth above. It is the Executive Branch that speaks as the voice of the United States with respect to foreign affairs and our diplomatic relations with the international community. That is why we urged Secretary of State John Kerry to recognize ISIS's atrocities as genocide against Christians. And that is why we will call upon the Executive Branch to follow through on our commitments at the U.N.

We will also call upon relevant Congressional Committees and Members of Congress to apply this same pressure, through appropriate channels, to the Executive Branch offices identified above. On this front, it is critical that Members of Congress hear from their constituents.

Sixth, call for the establishment of in-region "safe zones" for the genocide victims. This step reflects the duty to protect Christians victimized by ISIS, and continues the ACLJ's... policy... regarding the Syrian refugee crisis: "The creation of 'safe zones' addresses the need to protect the persecuted, while still protecting the national security interests of the United States."

Seventh, call for the creation of an effective international coalition to defeat ISIS militarily, for example, by expanding military efforts, changing the focus of the effort, and/or reevaluating the strategy of military action. We agree with Pope Francis, who has recognized that military force is justified to stop the genocide against Christians. The status quo is insufficient. This continues the ACLJ's... policy... regarding the Syrian refugee crisis: "We must destroy ISIS once and for all to provide a sustainable and lasting solution for the approximately 10 million refugees who have been displaced," many of whom are Christians or adherents to minority religious beliefs.[20]

We began implementing this plan piece by piece. We began analyzing the law. We began gathering information, much of which came directly from sources on the ground. We took the signatures of the hundreds of thousands of people who were signing our petitions and started sending them to world leaders. And each of our legal letters focused on a different aspect of our plan.

We are happy to report that, because the American people were willing to act, we saw either full implementation or significant progress toward each of these goals.

Our—and your—efforts had a monumental impact. Here's how we took your voice to the international stage.

CHANGING THE COURSE OF HISTORY—THE GENOCIDE RESOLUTION

Your voice secured what has become one of the most meaningful actions at the United Nations in defense of Christians and other religious minorities facing genocide at the hands of ISIS jihadists in Iraq.

It is the result of years of relentless work behind the scenes and on the world stage, culminating in a unanimous U.N. Security Council resolution specifically addressing ISIS's "genocide."[21] It is a major step forward in implementing the first (recognition of genocide), third (prosecution), and fourth (activation of the international community in protecting Christians) prongs of our seven-point plan.

This progress was the first step in what will be a long process to protect Christians and other religious minority victims of genocide, but without your voice it wouldn't have been possible. The silent screams of hundreds of thousands of dying Christians would never have been heard.

For more than six and a half years, the ACLJ has been working to draw attention to the plight of Christians in Iraq and Syria and to secure their protection.

We did so through emails, blogs, and on our daily radio broadcast. We have focused our international legal advocacy on a simple, two-part clarion call: (1) recognize the genocide and (2) protect Christians and other religious minorities.

We have engaged in efforts to mobilize the appropriate authorities in the United States and in the international community to end the ISIS genocide against Christians and other religious minorities and to bring relief and protection to ISIS's victims.

Many of you have partnered with us during these challenging years, signing petitions, sharing on social media the plight of Christians facing genocide, and adding your voices to our legal letters. Your voices and our work are making an impact.

Our legal advocacy campaign against ISIS genocide began soon after the formation of ISIS in April 2013. Our legal efforts—combined with public support and petition signatures— are effecting change.

We want to show you how our efforts—your voice—are changing policy at the United Nations. Here are some real-life examples that show how the engagement of thousands of people like you is already making a difference:

In April 2016, the ACLJ sent a letter to then–U.N. secretary-general Ban Ki-moon, requesting that the world body formally recognize that the ongoing atrocities committed by ISIS against Christians in Iraq and Syria constituted genocide. Here is part of what we said:

> The United Nations must stand against the evils of the ongoing genocide and use all available options to stop the genocide and protect the victims—by implementing appropriate penal tribunals, coordinating a more effective use of coalition military force, administering a more efficient delivery of aid, and providing meaningful in-region protection for victims

such as the establishment of safe-zones. The Charter of the United Nations demands no less, and through the organs of the United Nations, equipped and empowered by the Genocide Convention, the United Nations has the unique capability to end the genocide and protect the Christians and other religious and ethnic minorities victimized thereby.[22]

Shortly after the ACLJ sent that letter, the U.N. secretary-general's special representative and head of the United Nations Assistance Mission for Iraq issued a report to the U.N. Security Council calling on the international community to "take steps to ensure the accountability of members of [ISIS] for the atrocious crimes they have committed" and promote stability in the areas that were liberated from ISIS forces.[23]

In another effort to engage the United Nations, we sent a letter[24] to each of the forty-seven member states of the U.N. Human Rights Council, asking for them to support the naming of ISIS's actions as "genocide" at the council's June 2016 meeting. Some of the member states we contacted did indeed reference the genocide, just as we had urged them to do.

Then, in August 2016, the ACLJ submitted a letter to Adama Dieng, the U.N. secretary-general's special adviser for the prevention of genocide, specifically in furtherance of the second prong (activating the special adviser) of our seven-point plan. We asked him to encourage the United Nations to formally recognize the ongoing atrocities committed by ISIS against religious minorities in Iraq and Syria as genocide. And we asked him "to urge the United Nations to declare that the acts committed by the Islamic State are genocide against Christians and other religious minorities, and to advocate and mobilize for action to halt the genocide without delay."[25]

From our previous work, we knew that many U.N. bodies can

influence decision making. So, through our European affiliate, the ECLJ, we sent a letter to every member of the U.N. Security Council in November 2016. We reminded the Security Council that the Charter of the United Nations demands that it do everything in its power to stand against genocide and protect the victims. We also implored each member to call for the council first to recognize the genocide, and then to "vocalise [their] support for a referral by the Security Council to the International Criminal Court *or the establishment of a competent tribunal in order to investigate violations by the Islamic State committed in Iraq, Syria, and elsewhere in the region against Christians.*"[26]

We then sent a legal letter to Iraq's ambassador to the United States, Fareed Yasseen. In that letter we

respectfully urge[d] [him] to make whatever demands or submissions necessary to the United Nations to initiate and request the international community to honor its commitments and obligations under the Convention on the Prevention and Punishment of the Crime of Genocide. Further, we respectfully request[ed] that [he] provide to us any suggestions on ways we may assist Iraq in mobilizing the international community to end the horrific and deadly acts of genocide and aid and protect the victims.[27]

This letter to Iraq proved key in helping us secure the monumental resolution at the U.N. Security Council. We'll show you how it happened, and how committed and strategic advocacy can and does get results.

In April 2017, we sent a letter to the United Nations' newly elected secretary-general, António Guterres. Our letter reiterated our previous correspondence to his predecessor, and requested that the new secretary-general declare the atrocities committed by ISIS against Christians as genocide, because "a declaration by your office that the Islamic State is engaged in genocide and a request by your office for the United Nations General Assembly (and other appropriate organs of the United Nations) to follow suit would carry significant weight."[28]

A few months later, in July of 2017, we sent another letter to the U.N. secretary-general's special adviser for the prevention of genocide, Adama Dieng, urging him to "press all relevant U.N. bodies, including the Security Council and the Human Rights Council" to "recognise the ongoing atrocities as genocide... [and] to take the steps necessary to halt the genocide and fulfill its responsibility to protect those victimised."[29]

Here, again, we pleaded with him to use the influence of his office to get the United Nations to act. We outlined two ways that the Security Council could begin to take action to comply with the "responsibility to protect" doctrine, which obligates individual states and the international community to protect people from genocide.

First, Iraq could request help from the Security Council, and second, the international community could take action if Iraq could not.

As you will see below, the special adviser for the prevention of genocide then shared this information with the appropriate officials in Iraq, which led to Iraq's eventual request to the U.N. Security Council. This is precisely what we had wanted him to do.

Two weeks later, we sent a letter to the government of the United Kingdom and other key world leaders informing them of the numerous atrocities that ISIS had committed against Christians and other religious minorities in Iraq and Syria, and of the imperative need for the "international community [to] join together to stop [the] growing threat."[30] We urged them to take action.

The Prime Minister's Office (10 Downing Street) responded

within days.[31] And then, about two weeks later, we received a more detailed response from the United Kingdom's Foreign and Commonwealth Office. The momentum had begun. In his letter, the minister of state for the Middle East and North Africa thanked us for our letter, and affirmed:

I share your anger at the human suffering of Christians, Y[a]zidis and other minorities in Iraq, Syria and the wider Middle East, many of whose communities have been devastated at the ends of [ISIS]. I want to see Christians and other minorities continuing to live, worship, and prosper in the Middle East. We are doing all we can to make this happen— providing humanitarian assistance to all those who need it, including minority communities and consistently underlining with the region's political leaders the importance of upholding freedom of religion and belief.[32]

Further responding to our call for action at the United Nations, the U.K. minister's letter outlined a campaign both to bring the perpetrators of genocide to justice and to protect the victims. It concluded, "We are working with our international partners, in particular the Government of Iraq, to bring a proposal at the UN to put the campaign into action."[33] Again, this is exactly what we had wanted them to do.

That promise—made in response to our call to action—would become Security Council Resolution 2379, which was adopted unanimously (more about it shortly).

As we pressed forward with our plan, we began gaining even more momentum. The next month, September 2017, we received a response letter from the U.N. secretary-general's special adviser for the prevention of genocide, Dieng, who acknowledged our call to action:

The call for accountability is a call I have made not only to Member States at the United Nations but also in my meetings with Iraqi authorities. I have highlighted the important contribution to reconciliation. I have also reiterated that taking *steps towards accountability is critical* to demonstrating that all populations will have a place in the future of Iraq, including ethnic and religious minorities.[34]

He went on to tell us that he had given our policy proposals to the Iraqi government:

In the absence of accountability processes at the national level, the international community can explore *the options that you set out in your letter*, some of which can also be initiated by the Government of Iraq. *I have personally shared these options with the Minister of Foreign Affairs of Iraq.*[35]

We learned that, after Dieng received our letter and shared that information with Iraq, the minister of foreign affairs of the Republic of Iraq sent a letter in August 2017 to the U.N. secretary-general and the Security Council requesting that they "ask the international community to provide assistance, so that [Iraq] can make use of international expertise in [its] effort to prosecute the terrorist entity [ISIS]."[36] The momentum was growing.

And then, shortly thereafter, both Iraq and the United Kingdom (which you will recall had responded to our call for action at the United Nations) cosponsored a critical U.N. Security Council resolution, Resolution 2379, which passed on September 21, 2017. That resolution empowered

the Secretary-General to establish an Investigative Team, headed by a Special Adviser, to support domestic efforts to hold [ISIS] accountable by collecting, preserving, and storing evidence in Iraq of acts that may amount to war crimes, crimes against humanity and genocide committed by the terrorist group [ISIS] in Iraq, to the highest possible standards...to ensure the broadest possible use before national courts, and complementing investigations being carried out by the Iraqi authorities, or investigations carried out by authorities in third countries at their request.[37]

Moreover, Resolution 2379 specifically acknowledged Iraq's August letter to the U.N. secretary-general and the Security Council requesting such assistance. It was clear that the U.N. Security Council took action because Iraq had asked for help.

Our letters to the U.N. secretary-general, the U.N. Security Council, Iraq, the U.K., and the U.N. special adviser for the prevention of genocide, followed by the unanimous passage of Resolution 2379, show how *persistent* advocacy can work.

The United Nations has taken the first step toward recognizing the genocide against Christians—the collection of evidence. This evidence will be used to bring to justice the perpetrators of the genocidal acts that have been committed against Christians and others.

Further, it shows the successful implementation of prongs one (recognition of genocide) and three (prosecution) of our plan, as evidence is collected for these two purposes. It also shows the implementation of prong two (activation of the special adviser on genocide).

But our work was not done. We sent a follow-up letter to the U.N. secretary-general calling on him to immediately implement the terms of the unanimous Security Council resolution.[38]

In a letter to Dieng, we offered to connect him and the secretary-general with individuals and groups in Iraq already doing the painstaking but critical work of collecting and preserving evidence of genocide.[39]

Getting the United Nations to recognize the genocide for what it was, and to do something about it, was just part of the process. There were other things that needed to happen. So we seized the momentum and followed up this initial victory with another critical victory: providing aid for Christians returning to their homes.

NAMING AND DEFEATING THE ENEMY

One of the first actions of the Trump administration was to retool the fight against ISIS. As we articulated in part seven of our seven-point plan, the only way to protect Christians was to defeat ISIS. The Trump administration first of all made the decision to call the enemy by its name—ISIS—something we had urged our government to do from the beginning. The only way to defeat the enemy is to know the enemy, to define the enemy.

The Trump administration then moved to annihilate the enemy's forces. And annihilate them they did. Increasing our military presence and cooperation with our allies, changing strategy and rules of engagement, and increasing bombing, air strikes, and other shows of military force are just a few of the ways they turned around the fight against ISIS.

Much of the credit goes to President Trump, who acted decisively, unleashing on ISIS the righteous might and power of the U.S. military. In doing this, he delivered on a promise he had made during his campaign—a promise countless pundits and critics said could never be fulfilled. President Trump's military strategy is the complete opposite of the Obama administration's failed appeasement strategy—a foreign policy failure we denounced for years.

This has been just one of the changes we have seen under the Trump administration. And it is working.

The contrast between the administrations is stark. For example: After the Obama administration recognized the "genocide," we grew frustrated because, as best we could tell, nothing real was being done to end it. Recognition of the reality on the ground was a critical first step, but it seemed like the next step never came. So we sent a FOIA request to the Obama State Department demanding proof that they were taking action, and when they did not respond as required by the law, we took them to federal court—litigation we've continued against the Deep State.

After reviewing the records they finally provided after we filed our lawsuit, we discovered that the Obama administration never had a plan to implement the Genocide Convention. The conclusion was easy to draw—it was calling it genocide merely to get us and the American people off its back. That didn't work. And over the last several years, we and the American people have forced a change—albeit a slow one.

This change highlights the contrast between the administrations. Now the Trump administration is taking steps to implement the Genocide Convention, fulfilling part five (implementation of Genocide Convention) of our seven-point plan.

PROVIDING CRITICAL AID FOR CHRISTIANS

In what may be the biggest step forward in our genocide campaign since the United States officially recognized the "genocide against...Christians" and the U.N. Security Council adopted Resolution 2379, the U.S. government has secured a critical concession from the United Nations, wherein relief aid could be delivered directly to Christians and other religious minority victims of genocide in Iraq—something we had been aggressively advocating from the beginning. This is a *major* step forward in implementing part four (activation of the international community in protecting Christians) of our seven-point genocide plan.

In keeping with that part of our plan, many of our letters to key figures within the international community focused on "urging recognition and declaration of the atrocities committed by ISIS against Christians as genocide, **in order to trigger the provisions of the Genocide Convention and provide relief and aid to religious minorities facing genocide.**"[40]

In July of 2017, we sent letters to twelve nations, ten of which—including the United Kingdom—had been directly affected by the ISIS terror and genocide. We urged these world leaders to pressure the United Nations to provide relief for the victims:

> The United Nations must stand against the evils of the ongoing genocide and use all available options to stop the genocide and protect the victims—by implementing appropriate penal tribunals, coordinating a more effective use of coalition military force, **administering a more efficient delivery of aid**, and providing meaningful in-region protection for victims such as the establishment of safe-zones.[41]

In August of 2017, the United Kingdom's minister of state for the Middle East and North Africa, Alistair Bart, responded to our letter and embraced our proposal:

> I share your anger at the human suffering of Christians...in Iraq, Syria and the wider Middle East, many of whose communities have been devastated at the hands of [ISIS]. **I want**

to see Christians and other minorities continuing to live, worship and prosper in the Middle East. We are doing all we can to make this happen—**providing humanitarian assistance to all those who need it, including minority communities** and consistently underlining with the region's political leaders the importance of upholding freedom of religion and belief.[42]

Then, in September of 2017, through our ECLJ office, we went to the U.N. Human Rights Council and delivered an oral intervention on behalf of the victims of genocide:

The UN must stand against the ongoing genocide by implementing appropriate penal tribunals, coordinating a more effective use of coalition military force, **administering a more efficient delivery of aid**, and providing meaningful **in-region protection for victims** such as the establishment of safe-zones. The Charter of the United Nations demands no less.[43]

You see, your voice is being heard. The world is listening. More important, world leaders are taking action.

We were elated when, during a speech to a Christian human rights organization in October of 2017, Vice President Mike Pence unveiled plans for a new policy that would provide aid directly to the persecuted Christians in Iraq:

We will no longer rely on the United Nations alone to assist persecuted Christians and minorities in the wake of genocide and the atrocities of the terrorist groups.... The United States will work hand in hand from this day forward with faith-based groups and private [organizations] to help those who are persecuted for their faith. This is the moment, now is the time, and America will support these people in their hour of need.[44]

The Trump administration is delivering on this promise, and Christians recovering from genocide in Iraq are now able to receive this much-needed aid.

But there's more. Initially, the United States Agency for International Development (USAID) announced that it would provide a $150 million blank check to the United Nations Development Programme (UNDP) for the vague purpose of helping "stabilize Iraq after liberation of areas held by the Islamic State of Iraq and Syria."[45] However, this arrangement provided no assurances that the aid would go to those who needed it the most—the victims of the ISIS genocide—making it an ineffective form of relief. And reports we were hearing from our friends on the ground bore out our concern.

Thankfully, the Trump administration has since negotiated a new deal—one that tracks closely with the policy position we advanced. The arrangement negotiated between the United States and the United Nations includes a requirement that the United Nations ensure that aid will directly "address the needs of vulnerable religious and ethnic minorities communities."[46]

USAID announced these new measures in a January 8, 2018, press release.[47]

According to President Trump's new deal as outlined in the 2018 USAID press release, USAID will give $150 million to the United Nations. Of that, USAID has already provided $75 million, with $55 million of that going specifically toward helping religious and ethnic minorities who are facing genocide by ISIS in Ninewa Province, which in Iraq is synonymous with Christians. Allocation of the additional $75 million will depend on the "UNDP's success in putting in place additional accountability, transparency, and due-diligence measures for the FFS." In other words, the Trump administration has told the United Nations that it must use our money to truly help the Christians, and the administration is holding them accountable to make sure that happens. Under the new arrangement, this money will directly go toward helping the victims and will assist in providing them with basic necessities "such as water, electricity, sewage, health and education."[48]

In an effort to ensure that these funds are used for their intended purpose—helping Christians, Yazidis, and other religious minorities—Tom Staal, a USAID counselor, said that USAID will be implementing oversight measures and even an agreement with the UNDP to allow the U.S. agency's inspector general to review the UNDP's books in order to provide for "more frequent, detailed reporting."[49]

Here is what all this means: nearly 75 percent of the U.S. funding provided thus far, administered through the United Nations, is to go directly to Christians and other minority victims of genocide. This is a major victory. It is also a massive step forward in accountability, as U.S. officials will have direct access to and oversight of the U.N.'s aid operations as they relate to Christian genocide victims. This has been severely lacking until now. Much of the aid that had been delivered was being diverted away from Christians. The Knights of Columbus described it as "the most positive American action on behalf of the[se] communities since 2003."[50] And indeed it is.

In fact, just weeks later, the government of the United Kingdom told us in a letter that it was following suit:

Alongside our continued commitment to bring [ISIS] to justice, we are using our aid budget to alleviate the immediate humanitarian suffering of the most vulnerable people in the region, including Christians, Y[a]zidis and other minorities, as well as the majority Muslim population in Iraq and Syria.[51]

As my dad, ACLJ Chief Counsel Jay Sekulow, explained:

The letter details how the UK is helping the situation by committing more than "£90 million [$117 million] in Conflict, Stability and Security Fund funding to Iraq, including over £25 million [$32 million] helping to make areas that have been affected by conflict safe...*so that civilians can return to their homes.*"

The UK has also continued to contribute to the U.N.'s Funding Facility for Stabilisation (FFS) in order to help fund "over 1,000 projects across Iraq, including over 250 covering health, education and electricity in the Nineweh Plains helping to jump-start local economies and provide vital support to Christian and other minority communities so they may flourish." This is critical because, as we noted in our letter, the Nineweh Plains are a major Christian area that has been brutalized by genocide....

This is the same U.N. fund—that will serve the same Christian area—through which the U.S. government has been instrumental in increasing aid to Christians in Iraq, implementing vital changes to the USAID program that we long advocated for.[52]

This is remarkable. Both the U.S. and UK governments are responding to you. They are taking action because people like you were willing to speak out and demand protection for Christians facing genocide.

Further, the Trump administration and several world leaders have positively responded on multiple occasions to our call for in-region safe zones (part six of our seven-point plan), providing a vital protection for Christians who have faced the worst genocide imaginable and only wish to return safely to their homes.

Again, these are only the first few steps in a long process. We are continuing to send new legal letters to keep the pressure on, and to ensure that these critical steps are implemented and that Christians and other religious minorities continue to return to their homes free of the threat of genocide that has long plagued the region. We will not stop fighting until, together, we are able to protect Christians and other religious minority victims of genocide. Your voice is being heard. Your voice will continue to be heard.

We know that we must all remain vigilant, as the jihadist plague continues to spread across the globe. We must remain watchful.

As you can see, the next red wave is about far more than just voting. We achieved massive change even when the leaders in office had to be dragged kicking and screaming all the way to action. But the right administration can make a world of difference. It can mean the difference between inaction and action. This is why we fight day in and day out at the ACLJ. It's all connected: domestic policy, foreign policy. The leaders we choose set the agenda. If we want leaders who care about our issues, we have to act to bring about the next red wave.

CHAPTER 10

FIGHTING FOR LIFE AND WINNING: DEFEATING THE ABORTION DISTORTION

THERE IS ANOTHER GENOCIDE, and it's occurring right here in America. More than 60 million lives have been lost. It is the leading cause of death in America—almost as many as the next two (heart disease and cancer)... *combined.*

It is abortion. The ultimate act of oppression and tyranny on the most innocent human life imaginable.

Nearly a million defenseless unborn babies are ruthlessly slaughtered each year in this country. More than 332,000 are aborted annually by Planned Parenthood alone. They are poisoned. They are ripped limb from limb. They are killed in ways too awful to put into words.[1]

Yet the horrendous act of abortion is not only tolerated, it is also *celebrated* by the Democrat Party. We've said it many times. The Left worships at the altar of abortion.

Theirs is a near-religious devotion to this barbaric act of killing a helpless child. The Left is obsessed with abortion.

Don't believe us? Think we're overstating the point? Consider this:

Democrats don't just run on a pro-abortion platform. As an aside, "pro-choice" is a complete mockery. There is no choice—

only abortion. Whenever a state attempts to pass laws to give women the information they need to make informed choices, the pro-choice lobby always challenges those laws in court, thereby preventing women from making any kind of informed choice.

ABORTION IS THE DEMOCRAT PARTY'S NUMBER ONE PRIORITY

The first bill proposed, voted on, and passed by Nancy Pelosi's brand-new Democrat-controlled U.S. House of Representatives after the 2018 midterm elections included not one, but two, provisions to expand taxpayer funding for abortion.

The first provision was to repeal President Trump's expanded Mexico City Policy. In its simplest terms, the policy prohibits U.S. taxpayer dollars from paying for abortions internationally. The provision to repeal it—passed as part of a larger bill under the cover of an attempt to end the government shutdown—would have directly funded abortions carried out overseas with our taxpayer dollars. The second provision would have *expanded* U.S. taxpayer funding for the United Nations Population Fund, which notoriously funds and promotes abortion.

Not just abortion, but taxpayer funding for abortion, was literally the Nancy Pelosi–led Congress's very first priority. Within two weeks of taking power in the House, the Democrats had introduced two more stand-alone bills to end the Mexico City Policy and statutorily repeal the Hyde Amendment, which prohibits taxpayer dollars from being used to directly fund abortions (with limited exceptions) domestically.

Again, abortion and taxpayer funding for abortion are priority number one for the Left.

As we've said so many times, the Left is relentless in pursuing its priorities. It will stop at nothing to push its radical pro-abortion agenda on the American people.

Another example of the Left's obsession with killing babies surfaced in the aftermath of the 2018 elections: In 2018, Democrats took complete control of the New York State legislature and the governor's mansion. What was their number one priority? You guessed it. Abortion. The New York legislature passed and Governor Andrew Cuomo signed a bill in early 2019 that essentially legalized abortion *up until the moment of birth.*[2]

Remember what celebrated neurosurgeon and President Trump's secretary of housing and urban development Dr. Ben Carson said: "As a surgeon, I have operated on infants pre-birth. I can assure you that they are very much alive."[3] Which side do you believe? A celebrated neurosurgeon who has operated on unborn children or New York politicians whose campaigns are funded by Planned Parenthood?

As CBS News put it, "Senate Republicans contended a bill backed by Cuomo would expand access to abortions later in pregnancy, and they managed to stymie the legislation until Democrats picked up eight seats in the recent election to take control of the 63-seat chamber."[4]

Cuomo waited until his party had won the state senate in the 2018 elections; then he went to work. But he didn't do it alone: "Former Secretary of State Hillary Clinton joined New York Gov. Andrew Cuomo on Monday in calling for codifying abortion rights in New York state law as a bulwark against any potential court challenges to the landmark *Roe v. Wade* decision made 46 years ago this month,"[5] CBS News reported. Flanked by Clinton, Cuomo vowed not to sign the state's budget unless the legislature passed the radical abortion law, which included the right to kill children up to the moment of birth.[6] As CBS News reported, "Clinton, appearing with the governor at a rally at Barnard College in Manhattan, said the Senate and Assembly, which are now both controlled by Democrats, should waste no time in approving the legislative packages."[7] Hillary Clinton in the thick of late-term abortion even after her 2016 defeat—she could have been the president.

My dad has often said that elections have consequences. And we are here to tell you: elections have consequences.

New York's baby-killing law is one of the most expansive and barbaric abortion laws any state has ever passed. And to celebrate the new victory won by the Left's culture of death, Governor Cuomo had One World Trade Center lit up with pink lights.[8]

Wait a minute.

One World Trade Center exists only because approximately three thousand people lost their lives in one day during a savage, nation-altering terrorist attack on September 11, 2001. Yet, on average, three thousand people lose their lives every single day to abortion.[9] And that's how the Democrats celebrate abortion— they light up the monument that was built as a memorial to the three thousand people who lost their lives.

That's how sick and twisted the Left is. It really is worshiping at the altar of abortion.

Planned Parenthood quickly tweeted: "This. Is. Huge."[10] The ACLU's New York chapter, which was present for the New York bill signing, explained:

These victories have been a long time coming. For years, these—and virtually all—progressive reforms have been stymied by the State Senate. But with the *progressive wave that swept the nation in November* and has brought new leadership to the State Senate, we're finally starting to see the change we've worked for for so long.[11]

That's what a "progressive wave" brings. Priority one is abortion.

And driving home the Left's march of death, Vermont[12] and Rhode Island[13] are in the process of passing similar laws. Others are sure to follow. In fact, a similar bill—stripping out any restrictions on abortion called the Repeal Act—has been proposed in Virginia and has the support of Virginia's Democrat governor, Ralph Northam.[14] Virginia's House of Delegates and Senate— both up for grabs in the 2019 election—have razor-thin conservative majorities. Virginia—which has far more restrictions on abortion than New York ever did—could follow the path paved by New York. Think about that. Just a few votes could erase all abortion restrictions in a state and allow abortions at any stage of pregnancy.

Abortion up to the moment of birth. Are you surprised? You shouldn't be. The Left is the party of partial-birth abortion. That's where they pull part of the baby outside the baby's mother before brutally ending the child's life. This kind of abortion was, in reality, on the ballot in the 2016 presidential election. Had Hillary Clinton and the Left won in 2016, what happened in New York could have happened in Washington. Remember Hillary Clinton's radical statements during the October 2016 presidential debate?

CHRIS WALLACE [*Fox News* anchor and political commentator]: I'm going to give you a chance to respond but I want to ask you Secretary Clinton, I want to explore how far you believe the right to abortion goes. You have been quoted as saying that the fetus has no constitutional rights. You also voted against a ban on late-term partial-birth abortions. Why?

HILLARY CLINTON: Because *Roe v. Wade* very clearly sets out that there can be regulations on abortion so long as the life and health of the mother are taken into account. And when I voted as a senator, I did not think that that was the case. The kinds of cases that fall at the end of pregnancy are often the most heartbreaking, painful decisions for families to make. I have met with women who, toward the end of their pregnancy, get the worst news one could get that their health is in jeopardy if they continue to carry to term or that something terrible has happened or just been discovered about the pregnancy. I do not think the United States government should be stepping in and making those most personal of decisions. So you can regulate if you are doing so with the life and health of the mother taken into account.

CHRIS WALLACE: Mr. Trump your reaction and particularly on this issue of late-term partial-birth abortion.

DONALD TRUMP: I think it's terrible if you go with what Hillary is saying in the ninth month you can take the baby and rip the baby out of the womb of the mother just prior to the birth of the baby. Now you can say that that's okay and Hillary can say that that's okay, but it's not okay with me. Because based on what she's saying and based on where she's going and where she's been, you can take the baby and rip the baby out of the womb on the ninth month on the final day. And that's not acceptable.[15]

Yes, elections have consequences. For good or ill, elections have consequences. The consequences in New York? They might as well have legalized child sacrifice, because this is no better.

Think we are overstating? If you have a child; if you've felt that baby move in the womb, kick, or respond to touch; if you've seen an unborn baby on an ultrasound; or if you've lost a baby to miscarriage, you know an unborn baby is a living, defenseless human being. And if you have not experienced any of that firsthand, you know how to Google. You've seen the pictures. You've read the Facebook posts.

You know. You know what New York has done is wrong. John Piper, the founder and leader of desiringGod.org, was right: we all know.[16] The time for pleading ignorance, the time for uncertainty—real or feigned—has long since passed.

In our line of work, we are often amazed at the religious-like zeal displayed by the pro-abortion Left. And it's not just in New York. Just how religiously dedicated is the Left to abortion?

Here's just one example: A few years ago, when Texas passed a bill to ban abortions after twenty weeks' gestation, the state legislature was forced to shut down temporarily because a crazed pro-abortion mob made it impossible to conduct business on the floor of the chamber. And what were they shouting in their attempt to defeat the restriction on abortion? "Hail Satan!"[17] We are not making this up. The Baals are in our midst and they are no longer cloaked; and the sickening practice of child sacrifice is happening here—and their cult of death is politically organized and active. Are we?

The abortion industry has deceived many over the years. Its practitioners have exploited women for money and profit. They've made millions in the shadows. Like skilled merchants, they've cashed in on the once-gray fog of uncertainty over when life begins. They've peddled their wares like charlatans.

But now they are *celebrating* killing the most innocent human life that exists—babies—and killing them up to the moment of birth. What New York did is just short of legalizing and promoting what Kermit Gosnell did in his "House of Horrors"[18]— killing babies born alive after botched abortion procedures. That's not deception anymore. That's outright evil on parade.

THE LEFT'S SUPREME COURT ABORTION HYSTERIA

There is no starker example of the Left's undying devotion to the culture of death than the most recent battles over President Trump's nominees for the Supreme Court. The radical Left's adherents have lost their minds in their shrill hysteria over the President's picks.

As many news outlets have reported and opined, the efforts by New York and other states to expand abortion rights is the Left's response to President Trump's Supreme Court appointees, Justices Neil Gorsuch and Brett Kavanaugh.

We were there when the Senate confirmed them. We were also there when members of the Left tried to block their appointments by making them out to be among the worst human beings on the planet.

It didn't matter then that the outrageous allegations against Kavanaugh would be disproven and one even recanted when held to the fire. Back then, in that moment, those allegations were treated by so many as if they were, more likely than not, the truth. Outlandish, crackpot allegations. Things too embarrassing to repeat. But they were repeated, all right. The mainstream, leftist, out-of-control media repeated them as if they were the undeniable truth. They *had* to stop someone who might not be a Planned Parenthood puppet.

The Left mobilized in a way that, unfortunately, only the Left seems able to do. Their supporters trotted out everyone from movie stars to crazies in costumes. They carried signs, they made up chants, and they had loudspeakers. One poster, plastered on a mailbox just outside the front door of our Washington office, read: "Roe v. Wade is more popular than Brett Kavanaugh."

Egged on by Democrat Party leadership and rank-and-file alike, they reportedly had buses transporting paid protesters[19] to cause a scene and generate news coverage. And they were successful…at least with causing a scene and generating news coverage.

We had a unique vantage point from our office on Capitol Hill just across the street from the Supreme Court and the Senate office buildings.

We were there, trying to get down Constitution and Pennsylvania Avenues to meetings by the White House, then having to wait while leftist mobs blocked the streets on their way to the Senate hearings. We were there in the Senate Judiciary Committee hearings that ran late into the evenings. We saw the commotion. We heard the orchestrated outbursts during the hearings. We witnessed the protests firsthand. We would walk into a hearing and see the people who were there to interrupt waiting in the "public" area of the audience. We could see who they were, in the lines to get in. And, like clockwork, every few minutes during the hearing, they would jump up, yell their absurdities, and wave their signs. Then they'd be ushered— forcefully at times—to the exit. Watching the spectacle unfold, it became obvious that their actions had been scripted. Someone wrote that script, you know. And it wasn't "moderates." It sure wasn't conservatives.

Regardless, and in spite of all their organized efforts, President Trump held strong, and to their credit, Senate Republicans held strong as well. We got the nominees through. According to some, we now have a pro-life majority on the Supreme Court. That remains to be seen. But if the rabid opposition unleashed by Planned Parenthood and others on the Left—especially against Justice Kavanaugh's confirmation—is any clue, *they* see these Supreme Court justices as a threat to their monopoly on unborn children. That tells us all we need to know.

But the rabid hysteria of those on the Left in these confirmation hearings not only failed to derail their confirmations in the Senate, but it also took a toll in the court of public opinion. They were exposed for what they really are—pro-abortion zealots. The American people are beginning to see through their "pro-choice" facade.

While the Democrat Party has shown an unwavering devotion to abortion at any cost, Republican politicians have generally, over time, been far less resolute in their defense of life. The only time we ever see a supposedly pro-life Democrat vote in favor of life is when it doesn't matter—when the vote is already assured to fail. Conversely, the only time moderate Republicans, who talk a pro-life game when necessary to get elected, vote against life is when it *does* matter. That's why the Republicans couldn't defund Planned Parenthood when they had a majority in the Senate and needed just fifty votes. Just fifty. And they couldn't, or wouldn't, do it.

We must stand up for life. We must speak for those who cannot speak for themselves. Unborn children don't get to vote. They don't get to lobby. They don't get to rally on the National Mall and demand equal rights. We must.

But while the deck may feel stacked against us—with the Left dedicated to death and Republicans failing to hold the line for life—there is hope. There are victories for life we can win.

But remember, elections have consequences, and we can show you how those consequences—if we elect the right people—can, in fact, be good for life.

VICTORIES FOR LIFE

Much as we explained in the last chapter, part of bringing about the next red wave is using the tools we have at our disposal to bring about change—even in the most difficult political environments.

In January 2019, on the forty-sixth anniversary of *Roe v. Wade*:

> Thousands of anti-abortion activists, including many young people bundled up against the cold weather gripping the nation's capital, gathered at a stage on the National Mall Friday for their annual march in the long-contentious debate over abortion.
>
> Signs reading "Choose love, Choose life," "I am the pro-life generation," and "Defund Planned Parenthood" dotted the crowd gathering under hazy, wintry skies at the morning rally.[20]

It wasn't just "thousands," as *USA Today* and many other mainstream media outlets reported. It was more like a hundred thousand.[21] As far as the numbers go, we stood outside our office on Capitol Hill at the conclusion of the March for Life. The sheer number of people who passed by our office—waving at us, smiling and encouraging us to continue our work—was breathtaking, even emotionally and spiritually moving. In our view, a hundred thousand was more like a minimum count of those in attendance that day.

Demonstrating the difference an election can make, Vice President Mike Pence addressed the crowd in person, as he had done the year before. And President Trump again conveyed a video message:

> "I am supporting the US Senate's effort to make permanent the Hyde Amendment, which prohibits taxpayer funding for abortion in spending bills. Today, I have signed a letter to

Congress to make clear that if they send any legislation to my desk that weakens the protection of human life, I will issue a veto. And we have the support to uphold those vetoes," he said.[22]

At the rally, the Trump administration highlighted some of its accomplishments for life in just its first two years in power. These truly are victories for life that should be celebrated.

According to a 2019 Department of Health and Human Services (HHS) news release issued in conjunction with the March for Life, Secretary Alex Azar stated:

"Promoting the dignity of human life from conception to natural death is one of the very top priorities of President Trump's administration. At HHS, through our work in healthcare, human services, public health, and biomedical science, we are committed to this effort. This means not just protecting human life in the administration of our programs, but also respecting the conscience rights of those who participate in HHS-funded programs. Under President Trump, HHS will continue to advance science and improve the health of Americans while protecting our most fundamental freedoms: the right to life and the right of conscience."[23]

What is most remarkable is that HHS, which has consistently been the most pro-abortion federal agency, is now leading the Trump administration's fight for life. Here are the Trump administration's pro-life accomplishments, made possible because of your vote in the 2016 presidential election, and described in this January 18, 2019, HHS memorandum:

TRUMP ADMINISTRATION ACTIONS TO PROTECT LIFE AND CONSCIENCE

- In February 2018, HHS updated its five-year Strategic Plan for 2018–2022, which highlights that a core component of HHS's mission is the dedication to protecting the life of all Americans at every stage of life, beginning at conception.

TITLE X REFORMS

- **New Title X Proposed Regulation:** In June 2018, HHS proposed a new Title X regulation that would enforce statutory program integrity provisions by no longer permitting Title X-funded family planning services at the same location where abortion is provided. HHS looks forward to issuing the final rule promptly.
- **Broadening Participation in Title X:** In its most recent Title X grant awards, HHS funded 12 organizations that were not current Title X grantees, including state health departments, a faith-based organization, and several community health centers.

PROTECTING CONSCIENCE

- **Enforcing Weldon & Coats-Snowe Amendments:** This week, the HHS Office for Civil Rights (OCR) notified the State of California that its law requiring pro-life pregnancy resource centers to refer clients for abortions, by posting notices about free or low-cost family planning services and abortion, violated the Weldon and Coats-Snowe Amendments. This is the first time that any state has been found in violation of these laws, reflecting HHS's heightened commitment to enforcing conscience protection statutes.

- **New Division to Protect Conscience and Religious Freedom:** In January 2018, OCR launched a new Conscience and Religious Freedom Division, the first time a federal office for civil rights has established a separate division dedicated to ensuring compliance with and enforcement of laws that protect conscience and free exercise of religion in healthcare and human services.
- **Protecting Conscience in Health Insurance:** In November 2018, HHS and the Departments of Labor and of the Treasury issued two final rules to provide regulatory relief to American employers, including organizations like the Little Sisters of the Poor, that have religious or moral objections to providing coverage for contraceptives, including those they view as abortifacient, in their health insurance plans. The departments are vigorously defending the final rules.
- **New Proposed Conscience Regulation:** HHS is in the process of finalizing a rule to strengthen enforcement procedures for 25 health-related federal conscience and religious freedom laws and enforce those laws as vigorously as other civil rights laws enforced by OCR. The proposed rule was issued in January 2018.

THE AFFORDABLE CARE ACT AND ABORTION

- **Separate Billing for Abortion Coverage:** In November 2018, HHS issued a proposed rule to require issuers of Qualified Health Plans—individual insurance plans under the Affordable Care Act (ACA)—to bill and send separate invoices for insurance coverage of non-Hyde abortions.
- **Ensuring Access to Policies without Abortion Coverage:** This week, HHS issued a proposed rule to require that insurance companies that offer ACA plans covering abortions of preg-

nancies that do not threaten the life of the mother or result from rape or incest must also offer at least one identical plan in the same geographic area that does not cover these abortions. (The rule would not apply in states with abortion coverage mandates.)

- **Hardship Exemption:** In April 2018, CMS issued guidance to allow individuals to claim a hardship exemption from the individual mandate if all affordable plans offered through the federal exchanges in an individual's area included abortion coverage, contrary to the individual's beliefs.

MEDICAID AND ABORTION

- **Rescinded Guidance that Limited States' Ability to Take Action Against Abortion Providers:** In January 2018, CMS rescinded April 2016 guidance that curtailed states' ability to set reasonable standards for determining which providers can participate in their Medicaid programs.

INTERNATIONAL STANCE ON LIFE

- **Changing the U.S. Message:** At international forums—such as the United Nations, the World Health Organization, and the Pan American Health Organization—HHS continues to fight the concept of abortion as a fundamental human right, as evidenced by statements, votes called, amendments offered, and resolutions opposed. The Trump administration does not recognize abortion as a method of family planning and refuses to fund abortion in global health assistance.
- **Protecting Life in Global Health Assistance:** HHS worked with the Department of State to implement President Trump's restored and expanded Mexico City Policy, now

known as "Protecting Life in Global Health Assistance," to ensure that, consistent with applicable law, global health assistance administered by HHS is not provided to foreign nongovernmental organizations that provide or promote abortion as a method of family planning.[24]

We've been working side-by-side with the administration, calling for, supporting, and preparing to help defend these significant pro-life policies. But were it not for the administration and groups like the ACLJ bringing this information to you, you would probably have never known that we are achieving real victories for life. The mainstream media surely wouldn't tell you.

This shows real progress, real changes, and real wins. It shows there is hope. It shows that the notion that "elections have consequences" can be a win, not just defeats. You voted for this. You'll need to vote for it again.

As for other wins, don't forget that Planned Parenthood President Cecile Richards resigned in 2018 amid allegations of and investigations into Planned Parenthood's unlawful acts in selling aborted babies' body parts for profit,[25] among other disturbing acts. As her tenure at Planned Parenthood was summarized by one report:

Under Cecile's leadership, Planned Parenthood has been exposed for refusing to report statutory rape and abuse, for aiding sex traffickers, for taking money to abort black babies, and for illegally profiting off of the body parts they have aborted. Ms. Richards leaves the organization just as the FBI is investigating likely criminal actions by the abortion giant.[26]

We can win.

But the victories have come not just from, or during, the Trump administration. We have been fighting and winning victories in the courts for years.

After California passed a shockingly unconstitutional pro-abortion law—the "Reproductive FACT Act"—that forced pro-life pregnancy centers to promote abortion, we filed a lawsuit. Pro-life pregnancy centers, or crisis pregnancy centers, as they are often called, serve women in need. They provide care, support, and assistance for pregnant women and their babies. They are a true alternative "choice" for pregnant women facing dire circumstances—a "choice" that Planned Parenthood and the rest of the supposedly "pro-choice" abortion industry would never offer. Now, these pro-life centers, whose very purpose was to promote life—not death, exploitation, and abortion—would be forced to promote the very thing they existed to oppose. They would be faced with crippling fines and penalties—and eventually a total shutdown—if they refused to comply with California's draconian law.

At the ACLJ, we exist, in part, to defend institutions like this that face the crippling power of the abortion industry and the coercive power of unconstitutional laws. We've fought similar laws in New York, Hawaii, and other states where the pro-abortion machine controlled the political players.

In California, the abortion lobby—NARAL Pro-Choice America—literally sponsored this law.[27] Their goal was to shut down the competition. You see, every life that a pro-life pregnancy center saves represents income that the abortion industry doesn't get—up to $1,500. By forcing pro-life centers to become walking advertisements for abortion, the abortion lobby not only silenced its competition, but they also actually forced its competition to be the abortion industry's ad agency.

It was one of the most anti–free speech laws we've ever seen, and it was cosponsored by none other than then California attorney general and now U.S. senator Kamala Harris.[28] Think about it: What if Pepsi could sponsor a law to force Coke to advertise for it? That could—and would—never happen. But, because of the abortion distortion, both the federal district court and the Ninth Circuit Court of Appeals ruled in favor of the abortion lobby and California. Pro-life centers were on the ropes. They were on the brink of being forced to close their doors under the threat of crippling fines and the strong arm of the government.

But we appealed our case, *Livingwell Medical Clinic v. Becerra*, to the Supreme Court, and others like us took similar cases out of California to the Supreme Court. We filed an amicus (friend-of-the-court) brief on behalf of hundreds of thousands of our members in the main case before the Court.[29]

We weren't the only ones who recognized the import of these cases. Here's what NARAL said:

This is the Supreme Court's first test on abortion rights with Neil Gorsuch on the bench, and the decision could set the stage for how courts treat abortion rights for decades to come.... As right-wing groups increasingly spread lies about abortion and basic reproductive healthcare, this case is an early test of whether the Supreme Court can guarantee our rights in the Trump era, including access to abortion care.[30]

In a way, they were right. This was a huge test. It would set the stage for how abortion cases will be decided for years to come.

But, thankfully, the abortion lobby didn't get its way in conscripting the pro-life movement to advertise, as unwilling foot soldiers, in its war on the unborn. In a landmark decision, the Supreme Court struck down the Reproductive FACT Act as unconstitutional.[31] Our clients' doors remain open.[32] We are now able to use the Supreme Court's decision in this case to secure victories in other states against similar anti-life laws. In fact, on the heels of this victory, we obtained a determination from HHS that the Reproductive FACT Act violated at least two federal statutes.[33]

This was a win from the top down. Our pro-life clients were fully vindicated. One of the worst pro-abortion laws we'd seen was struck down, giving us the tools—and precedent—we needed to dismantle similar laws nationwide.

It was made possible for three reasons: (1) President Trump was elected to nominate pro-life justices; (2) his pro-life nominees on the Supreme Court and at HHS fulfilled their constitutional duty, striking down this anti–free speech law; and (3) you and hundreds of thousands like you were willing to stand up to the abortion lobby. You stood up to the abortion industry. You would not back down.

These are the kinds of victories we can have on a variety of fronts, but the fights are fierce. The abortion lobby is creative in its evil. It will stop at nothing to expand its religious devotion to death. But it can be defeated. We must be willing to stand in the gap and fight back. We must be tenacious in the face of evil. There is too much at stake to be complacent. But to bring about the next red wave, we must open our eyes wide. We must understand the weapons the enemy will use against us if we are to be prepared for these fights.

One of the biggest weapons of death we face in the fight for life is what we call "the abortion distortion," but even that is something we can—and are—chipping away at.

THE ABORTION DISTORTION

In the legal world, "the abortion distortion" is a phrase used to describe what happens when the law is applied differently in a case involving abortion than in any other area. It means that the legal principles are shifted. The goalposts move. It's as if the same rules don't apply to abortion cases that apply to other cases. Everything changes when it comes to abortion. We've seen this in so many cases. It distorts the law, which is why we call it the abortion distortion.

Imagine in any sport if the rules were applied differently to one team than to all the others. Fouls were different; points were scored differently. This is exactly what happens with abortion cases.

It's the same way outside of the law, too. Whether it's politics, the media, or the law, abortion is treated differently.

Free speech is protected—unless it's pro-life speech. There are actually state and local laws passed that ban pro-life speech on public sidewalks, while allowing pro-abortion speech to occur on the same sidewalk. It's anathema to the First Amendment. It's absurd. But in many courts, this is treated as a perfectly reasonable restriction. At the ACLJ, we've been involved in a number of these cases at the Supreme Court over the years. Some we've won, others lost. Floating buffer zones (you can't speak in favor of life within a certain number of feet of another person) are not okay, but fixed buffer zones (you can't speak in favor of life within a certain number of feet from a building) are okay—unless it's too close or too far away, in which case, it's not okay. Confused?

Yeah, so are we. From the Supreme Court down to the district courts, cases involving abortion are treated differently. The same judges and justices will rule in opposite ways on a basic legal principle based on whether the underlying facts of the case involve abortion.

A recent case made this point crystal clear.

Supreme Court Justice Clarence Thomas, joined by Justices Samuel Alito and Neil Gorsuch, poignantly called out the abortion distortion. He did so in a little-covered dissent in a case the Supreme Court didn't even agree to hear that involved a state defunding Planned Parenthood from Medicaid reimbursements. The case raised an important legal question, there was a circuit split, and numerous states asked the Supreme Court to weigh in—really everything that makes for a Supreme Court case—but the Court refused to take it. Justice Thomas took the Court to task over why:

So what explains the Court's refusal to do its job here? I suspect it has something to do with the fact that some respondents in these cases are named "Planned Parenthood." That makes the Court's decision particularly troubling, as the question presented has nothing to do with abortion. It is true that these particular cases arose after several States alleged that Planned Parenthood affiliates had, among other things, engaged in "the illegal sale of fetal organs" and "fraudulent billing practices," and thus removed Planned Parenthood as a state Medicaid provider. But these cases are not about abortion rights. They are about private rights of action under the Medicaid Act. Resolving the question presented here would not even affect Planned Parenthood's ability to challenge the States' decisions; it concerns only the rights of individual Medicaid patients to bring their own suits.

Some tenuous connection to a politically fraught issue does not justify abdicating our judicial duty. If anything, neutrally applying the law is all the more important when political issues are in the background. The Framers gave us lifetime tenure to promote "that independent spirit in the judges which must be essential to the faithful performance" of the courts' role as "bulwarks of a limited Constitution," unaffected by fleeting "mischiefs." The Federalist No. 78, pp. 469–470 (C. Rossiter ed. 1961) (A. Hamilton). We are not "to consult popularity," but instead to rely on "nothing... but the Constitution and the laws." *Id.*, at 471.[34]

This is the abortion distortion. The laws apply differently. The rules of statutory construction apply differently. The Constitution applies differently. The justices treat it differently.

It explains how tattoo parlors are required to adhere to higher health and safety standards than abortion clinics.[35] It explains why the same people who want to regulate your kid's lemonade stand don't want any regulations on abortion. It explains why the law protects the eggs of some birds[36] more than unborn babies. It explains why some consent and ultrasound laws are struck down, but laws forcing pro-life centers to promote abortion are upheld (at least until we defeated one such law at the Supreme Court).[37] It explains why investigative journalists who expose horrendous conditions at meat packing plants are heralded, but investigative journalists who uncover Planned Parenthood's and the abortion industry's sale of aborted babies' body parts for profit are arrested and gagged from sharing the truth.[38]

Abortion has its own rules. They don't follow the Constitution. And they only go one way—in favor of abortion and against innocent life.

In this case, it doesn't just *feel* like the deck is stacked against life. The deck *is* stacked against life.

To win in a case involving abortion requires more than just

175

having the law on our side. We have to work twice as hard. That's because we're fighting the other team *and* the refs—which some sports fans understand very well.

But it can be done. As we've just shown, the fight for life is difficult, but it can be won.

It begins with recognizing the abortion distortion in all its many forms (something we hope this chapter helps you see). Then we have to act to counterbalance it.

Having a president who doesn't just say he's pro-life, but who is also willing to implement pro-life policies in his administration, makes a huge impact—an impact you can take some credit for because you put Donald Trump in the White House. The appointment of sincerely pro-life judges is also something that helps push back against the abortion distortion. He is doing that, too. And, giving credit where it is due, Senate Majority Leader Mitch McConnell, along with former Chairman Chuck Grassley's and now Lindsey Graham's Senate Judiciary Committees, have helped the President by confirming his nominees at a record pace.[39]

But the biggest thing we can do to cut through the abortion distortion is to continue to call it out each and every time it rears its ugly head. Whatever the arena; however well funded the opponent.

Just as Justice Thomas did, we must be willing to expose the illogic and transparent bias of the abortion distortion. Don't be silent. Don't allow the truth to be twisted and contorted. Don't be afraid to speak out. Push back against the abortion distortion. We do this each and every day at the ACLJ. And you can play a crucial role. By sharing our articles exposing Planned Parenthood, signing our pro-life petitions, and joining our briefs, you are helping us combat the abortion distortion.

Politically, unborn children are members of the most vulnerable class there is. They literally have no voice. They can join no labor union. They can join no political action committee (PAC). Speak for them. And speak loudly, because the abortion distortion goes beyond the courts and the legislatures; it is amplified by the mainstream media—much of which the President famously calls "fake news."

CHAPTER 11

FAKE NEWS

#FAKENEWS. I'm sure you've heard a lot about it. But what is it?

Is it some radical, tinfoil-hat conspiracy theory about how the corporate-industrial-complex-run media is colluding to bring about a new world order through propaganda? No. It's not.

Fake news, though it may sound ironic, is very real.

While the mainstream media would like you to believe that fake news is some crackpot Trump theory or that it is a war on the freedom of the press or that conservatives have concocted their own set of alternative facts, that is not at all what fake news is about.

For years, we've known that the liberal elites ensconced in the ivory towers of the mainstream media are biased. They've always slanted stories, relentlessly mocked conservatives (see Sarah Palin and the quote she never said, "I can see Russia from my house"),[1] and buried stories that didn't fit their narrative. It was simple bias.

No discussion of media bias would be complete without recognizing the role that early new media pioneers have played in calling out the media bias and stepping up to challenge its control over information. From radio talk show host and political commentator Rush Limbaugh's courageous stand against the Clinton Machine of the 1990s and what he called the "drive-by media" to Fox News talk show host and political commentator Sean Hannity's domination of cable television with bold and strikingly commonsense monologues, all now know that fake news has a competitor. The Media Research Center made its mark with statistics, fact checking, and its simple but poignant "Don't believe the liberal media" bumper sticker. Those were the pioneers in the fight over information. And we are right in the middle of the fray. The audience for my dad's daily radio show that I cohost, *Jay Sekulow Live*, now broadcasting on nearly one thousand stations and streaming audio and video online, has grown to reach millions.

But the forces driving fake news are smart, ruthless, and shameless. Fake news has evolved past simple bias, slanting or even burying stories those forces don't like. Now the fake news machine is willing to make things up to push its leftist agenda. Call it "Trump Derangement Syndrome," or call it the logical next step of liberal media bias running headfirst down a slippery slope in a race to the bottom; but whatever you call it, it should be repugnant to anyone who believes in a free press.

Fake news is what you get when the mainstream media doesn't tell the truth. It's that simple. Generally, two steps are involved in the creation of fake news:

Step One: Make up a news story that fits your preconceived narrative, either completely out of thin air or by omitting those parts of the story that do not support your narrative. Just make sure to include some unnamed sources to give your made-up story credibility.

Step Two: Eagerly repeat this made-up or manipulated story whenever possible. A lie repeated often enough becomes true.

Or, when necessary, fail to report on a story altogether. One of the greatest powers the mainstream media has is the power to ignore.

For extra credit, "responsible" journalists will use phrases like "if true" to provide cover and make it seem like they are exercising their due diligence as reporters. They are not. This is just expert-level fake news.

Devoting hours and even days to a made-up story, with serious facial expressions and stern tones, while occasionally sprinkling in a qualifier of "if true," is still devoting hours and days *to a made-up story*. That little two-word qualifier makes all the difference. It's like George Orwell's "newspeak." The term "if true" now means it is not true, but because the "Ministry of Truth" wants it to be true, you had better act like it is true.

What happened to journalistic integrity?

Responsible journalists report facts as facts. They don't make up facts. They don't try to instigate a reaction by those in power. They don't commentate. They investigate and they corroborate their stories. This used to be how the news media reported. True journalists' opinions were not supposed to matter. They made sure what they were reporting was factually accurate, and they reported the news. This was the hallmark of journalism. Reporting something that turned out to be false was fatal to a journalist's career. Their stock in trade was accuracy and credibility. And their credibility was based on whether what they reported was, in fact, true; not on whether people liked what they said.

Nowadays, the line between reporter and commentator has essentially been erased. There was supposed to be a difference between Sean Hannity (a commentator) and Jim Acosta, whose official title is chief White House correspondent for CNN, but it should be chief White House commentator.

It's not just the line between pundit and journalist that is now blurred; so, too, is the line between journalism and creative fiction writing. The shameful antics of "BuzzFeed News" provide a nice example. As we explain below, BuzzFeed literally made up a story about the Special Counsel's Office that was so abjectly false that the Mueller team had to publicly refute it.

For many mainstream media journalists, work is no longer about reporting facts. It has come to be about advancing narratives. They do not investigate facts and write stories about what they find. They start with a narrative and look for "facts"—regardless of whether they are true—that back up that narrative. If a given fact doesn't back up a narrative, it either doesn't get reported or is buried on page A13, at the end of the story. The salacious, unverified stuff is in the headline and above the fold on page A1. It's nothing more than glorified clickbait.

But twisting facts to fit a preconceived narrative doesn't represent the worst of fake news. That prize goes to those journalists who simply make up a story altogether. Here's how it works: Unnamed sources say the sky is falling, and the mainstream media echo chamber becomes a bunch of Chicken Littles running around. They breathlessly regurgitate falsehoods with impunity, only to move on to the next story when they are proven wrong. They don't verify. They don't name sources. And if one mainstream media source reports it, they all run with it, treating it as fact.

One of the first and most obvious examples of fake news occurred when Dan Rather, then a longtime anchor for *The CBS Evening News*, reported that documents had been discovered essentially proving that President George W. Bush had been AWOL during his service in the Texas Air National Guard. This became a massive scandal just weeks before the 2004 presidential election.[2] The reality was these documents were forgeries. They were fakes. Yet Rather reported them, and the rest of the mainstream media ran with the story. It fit their preconceived narrative that

President Bush was not worthy of the office he held and had run away from the fight when he was in the military.

The story that aired made him look bad. It helped the leftist challenger whom the journalists supported. It was also not true. It was false. Made up. Defamatory. Yet it was reported as absolute fact. It was fake news, and its creators attempted to use it to sway a presidential election.

Even just a few years ago, a fake news story could still cost a journalist his or her job. Rather was let go, though in today's standardless media landscape he is, unsurprisingly, mounting a comeback. Remember NBC's Brian Williams? He lost his anchor job after it was proven that he had lied about taking fire on a helicopter while reporting during the Iraq War. Yet he, too, is back on the air.

In the current, hyper-politicized media landscape, the mainstream media seems to reward purveyors of fake news more often than it punishes them.

But, of course, ratings, viewership, and readership are down. And many think the mainstream media's rabid hatred of then-candidate Donald Trump played a role in his surprising election—in other words, it backfired on them. Candidate Trump and we the people recognized the fake news for what it was and rebelled. It can happen again. The next red wave may depend on it.

THE BUZZFEED MICHAEL COHEN FAKE NEWS STORY

One of the better (well, worst) examples of fake news came from a shocking report courtesy of BuzzFeed News in early 2019. Late on a Thursday night, BuzzFeed posted an article headlined:

"President Trump Directed His Attorney Michael Cohen to Lie to Congress about the Moscow Tower Project."[3]

The piece cited "two federal law enforcement officials involved in an investigation of the matter." No names. The article's two authors were identified as BuzzFeed News reporters. Not opinion journalists, not advocates. But news reporters.

To the liberal elite mainstream media, this was too good to be true. They had finally uncovered the "smoking gun" in the Russia investigation that would bring down President Trump, if true. They had him, if true. This could be grounds for impeachment, if true. Of course, it was too good to be true, because it was not true.

It was 100 percent fabricated. False. Fake news.

But that did not slow down the machine. In less than an hour, other "news" outlets picked up the story and ran. MSNBC's headline:

"Trump told his lawyer Michael Cohen to lie to Congress about Russia Trump Tower deal, BuzzFeed report says."[4]

Axios read:

"BuzzFeed: Trump told Cohen to lie to Congress about Moscow tower."[5]

Here is CNN's opening paragraph from its version of the story:

President Donald Trump personally directed his longtime former attorney Michael Cohen to lie to Congress about the Moscow Trump Tower project, two federal law enforcement officials involved in an investigation of the matter told Buzz-Feed.[6]

See how credible CNN wanted its readers to think the story was? Look at the verbiage. Look at the sentence structure. This is a statement of fact. It is not until three paragraphs into the story that we learn that "CNN has not corroborated the Buzz-Feed report."[7] This, even though, when pressed by their media peers the following day, the two authors posing as news reporters gave conflicting information about whether they had even seen the documents themselves.

And just like that, for the next forty-eight hours, it was breath-lessly reported ad nauseam. It was the top story of every media outlet in the country. Not a single member of the mainstream media bothered to verify the report—*because they couldn't*. It wasn't true, so it couldn't be verified.

They just ran with it. Covered it. Commentated on it. They practically drew up articles of impeachment.

And then something truly shocking happened. The Special Counsel's Office, which until then had been silent on nearly every story, leak, and piece of fake news emanating from the media frenzy over the Russia investigation, actually refuted the entire story.

It's not just us saying the BuzzFeed story was wrong; the in-vestigators themselves did.

The special counsel's spokesman released a rare statement the next day disputing the fake news story piece by piece as "not ac-curate." The "news" outlets were forced to slip that statement into their articles—but they did not retract their earlier reporting.

According to the Special Counsel's Office:

BuzzFeed's description of specific statements to the Special Counsel's Office, and characterization of documents and tes-timony obtained by this office, regarding Michael Cohen's Congressional testimony are not accurate.[8]

184

That's three separate things about the article they refuted: (1) specific statements, (2) characterization of documents, and (3) testimony "are not accurate." Said another way, they are fake news.

This is astounding. Usually the fake news machine can get away with pulling a stunt like this. But not this time. They were caught red-handed. So they retracted the story, right? I mean they had to, right? No. They doubled down. That's how fake the fake news is.

In the not-too-distant past, such a direct denial by a federal law enforcement office would have ended careers. Embarrassed news executives would have retracted the faulty stories. Some might even have apologized. But that was then, and this is now. Now there is no shame.

And speaking of no shame, BuzzFeed has a track record. One that President Trump was right to call out when he tweeted:

Remember it was Buzzfeed that released the totally discredited 'Dossier,' paid for by Crooked Hillary Clinton and the Democrats (as opposition research), on which the entire Russian probe is based.[9]

Other outlets initially refused to publish the dossier, but reversed course and piled on once BuzzFeed chose to do so, on January 20, 2017. The dossier was the one that fired FBI director James Comey described later, in testimony to Congress, as "salacious and unverified"—while he was apparently using information contained in the dossier to justify signing Foreign Intelligence Surveillance Act (FISA) applications to spy on peripheral volunteer advisers to the Trump campaign.

The latest example regarding Cohen's testimony—refuted by the Special Counsel's Office itself—may have been fake news at its worst.

This should have been an embarrassment for the mainstream media—except they appeared not embarrassed, but merely disappointed that it wasn't true.

To us, it showed how toxic and unhinged the Left has become. How its members have infiltrated one of our most sacred institutions and exploited it for political gain. They don't care about the truth. They care about pushing their radical agenda.

Nowhere is this more obvious than when it comes to the abortion distortion.

THE 3 PERCENT LIE

One of the longest-running fake news stories is the 3 percent lie.

For years, Planned Parenthood—the largest abortion business in America—has hidden its true abortion agenda behind a 3 percent lie. The mainstream media has been all too willing to help Planned Parenthood spread its propaganda. It's where the abortion distortion meets fake news.

Planned Parenthood's lie is simple, "Three percent of all Planned Parenthood health services are abortion services."[10]

It's been repeated without end by willful abortion promoters and mindless commentators alike. It has been unquestioned. It has been the number one propaganda piece Planned Parenthood has perpetuated each and every time its abortion business and its half-billion dollars in annual taxpayer funding has been questioned.

Planned Parenthood is skillfully adept at accounting gimmicks (it was, after all, in the room[11] for the finalization of Obamacare, its abortion-pill mandate, and subsequent bogus "accommodation").

As we at the ACLJ have explained many times, Planned Parenthood unbundles all of its services except abortion to create a lopsided and deceptive view of them.

Here is what happens: Planned Parenthood claims to provide 9.7 million "services"[12] in America each year. From this inflated number, they calculate that the 332,757 abortions they reported in 2018[13] amounted to only 3.4 percent of their services.

Planned Parenthood's 2017–2018 report states that it performed "nearly 9.7 million services during 4 million clinical visits."[14] So the reality is that 8.3 percent of clinic visits were for abortions. That's right, 8.3 percent of all visits to Planned Parenthood result in an abortion. And that's up from 6.6 percent of clinical visits in past years.[15]

Dig a little deeper and you'll find that Planned Parenthood says that all those "services" go to just 2.4 million "patients." So, by its own admission, nearly 14 percent of the "patients" who visit a Planned Parenthood clinic in any given year obtain an abortion there (Planned Parenthood no longer reports the number of women it provides "services" to, so "patients" includes both men and women).

What about some of the other "services" Planned Parenthood claims it provides? Prenatal services (those services provided to women who choose to keep their baby) account for a pitiful 0.09 percent of all services provided. Think about that; not even one-tenth of 1 percent of services offered by Planned Parenthood go toward helping women *keep* a baby. Moreover, the 2,831 adoption referrals made by Planned Parenthood according to their 2017–2018 annual report amount to a whopping 0.029 percent of services rendered. In fact, adoptions referrals dropped by more than 27 percent in the previous year. Some "choice" they offer.

Again, these figures are deceptive. Planned Parenthood unbundles all of its other services so as to inflate its overall numbers. We caught them with their own numbers, which they have since stopped reporting. In 2009, Planned Parenthood reported performing 40,489 prenatal services[16] for 7,021 prenatal clients,[17] an average of roughly six services per prenatal client. Since 2009, they stopped reporting the number of prenatal clients and instead list only the larger prenatal services number.

But, assuming an average of six prenatal services per client, Planned Parenthood's current listing of 9,055 prenatal "services"[18] could be for just over 1,500 prenatal clients. That is 1,500 babies helped versus well over 332,000 babies killed.

Here's how we've explained it before:[19]

Planned Parenthood's claim that only 3 percent of its business is abortion is no different than if a car dealership claimed that it wasn't really in the business of selling cars because the number of new car sales was only a fraction of its total services provided (financing cars, repairing cars, providing manufacture recommended maintenance for cars, cleaning cars, and so forth). Of course no one would believe such an outrageous claim. Sure, a car dealership does all of those things, but its purpose is to sell cars.

The abortion industry is no different. The abortion industry, led by Planned Parenthood, is about committing abortion. Sure they provide some other services, but when your only self-sustaining revenue source is one thing and you are responsible for [somewhere between 28 and] 40 percent[20] of that one thing in the entire nation, that is what you are about. Planned Parenthood is about abortion.

According to Planned Parenthood's own apologist, Media Matters,[21] its "total revenue from abortion services was approximately $164,154,000," a year. Accordingly, over 51 percent of Planned Parenthood's clinic income comes from abortion.

Think about that. Half their clinic income could come from abortion, but the media reports that abortion is only 3 percent of what Planned Parenthood does.

While this is an example of one of the longest-running fake news stories out there, it is also an example of how you can defeat them.

It's really quite simple: the truth. But it takes embarrassing members of the media establishment to force them to report it.

For years, we've been repeatedly exposing Planned Parenthood's 3 percent lie and calling out the mainstream media for reporting it as fact. Finally, a few years ago, the fact checkers at the *Washington Post* reached out to us about our analysis. We walked them through our calculations step by step—similar to the way we explained them above—using empirical data and Planned Parenthood's own reports and price sheets to show them the unmistakable fact that Planned Parenthood was flat-out lying.

By presenting the truth in an irrefutable manner, we forced even the *Washington Post* to call out its own fake news—awarding three Pinocchios to the 3 percent lie.

Here's the crux of the *Washington Post*'s fact check:

> When all services are counted equally, abortion procedures do account for 3 percent of Planned Parenthood's total services.
>
> But there are obvious differences between these services. For example, a first trimester abortion can cost up to $1,500, according to the Planned Parenthood Web site. Yet an emergency contraceptive pill costs around $45 and a urine pregnancy test costs around $10 at a pharmacy. An abortion is a different type of procedure than a vasectomy, or testing for sexually transmitted infections or diseases, or a vaccine for human papilloma virus (HPV), and so forth.

While each service is listed separately, many clients received multiple services. A woman may get a pregnancy test, birth control and a pap smear, but she would be counted three times, once for each service, in the annual report.[22]

As we said at the time, referencing the *Washington Post*'s fact check analysis:[23]

Cutting through the blatant factual distortions painted by Planned Parenthood's deceptive 3% figure, WaPo uses Planned Parenthood's own statistics, much like [we] have in the past,[24] to expose the abortion giant's lies. It notes that according to Planned Parenthood's own data, "patients who received abortions would account for 12 percent of total patients," and "abortions comprised 14 percent of [Planned Parenthood clinic] visits."[25]

The *Washington Post* Fact Checker continues, noting, as [we] have in the past,[26] that looking at Planned Parenthood's abortion revenue could paint a far better picture of Planned Parenthood's true business model:

"Typically, this calculation is made by taking the number of abortions, multiplying them by the average cost of abortions advertised by Planned Parenthood clinics, and dividing the figure by the organization's total nongovernment health services revenue [clinic income].

The main Planned Parenthood Web site says first-trimester abortions can cost up to $1,500. Some affiliate clinic Web sites provide a range of costs: a Western Pennsylvania clinic lists $390 to $1,090 for abortions, and first trimester abortion is priced at $515 in Arizona."[27]

It explains that while "advocates and opponents of abortion rights have calculated somewhere between 15 percent [of

190

total revenue] and 37 percent [of clinic revenue]" comes from abortion, "depending on which price you use, you can even get up to 55 percent."[28]

That's 55% of Planned Parenthood's clinic income coming from abortion. [We]'ve previously calculated this at 51% of its clinic income.[29] It's clearly grown in recent years.

In the end, the *Washington Post* gives Planned Parenthood's longstanding 3% claim three Pinocchios (out of four), which according to its rating standard means that the claim [contains] "significant factual error and/or obvious contradictions."[30]

Our report concludes noting that the *Washington Post* rightly finds:[31]

"The 3 percent figure that Planned Parenthood uses is misleading, comparing abortion services to every other service that it provides. The organization treats each service—pregnancy test, STD test, abortion, birth control—equally. Yet there are obvious differences between a surgical (or even medical) abortion, and offering a urine (or even blood) pregnancy test. These services are not all comparable in how much they cost or how extensive the service or procedure is."[32]

Unsurprisingly, Planned Parenthood refused to comment and provide further data to the WaPo Fact Checker, further evidencing its nefarious intent.

As the *Washington Post* notes, "Planned Parenthood could end the speculation—and Pinocchios—by providing a more transparent breakdown of its clients, referrals and sources of revenues."[33] It is the one with all of that data—data that likely flies in the face of Planned Parenthood's bogus propaganda.

But of course Planned Parenthood won't do that (and in this case when given the chance, refused to do that). Planned Parenthood has been caught in a lie.

Except this time, instead of being dismissed as just another pro-life attack, Planned Parenthood has been exposed by one of its media elite allies.

We helped expose the fake news—defeat the fake news. Yet even after the *Washington Post* fact checker acknowledged the truth, most of the mainstream media still reports the 3 percent lie as fact. **In fact, the** *Washington Post* **itself still repeats**[34] **the 3 percent lie with no reference to its own fact check showing it is patently false.** Think about that. That's what we mean by fake news.

Planned Parenthood's propaganda is being boosted by the fake news media. Repeat a lie for long enough and it starts to become part of the public consciousness. That is fake news. But there are cracks in the fake news media.

We can now point to the *Washington Post* fact check piece each and every time the fake news media tries to regurgitate the same fake news 3 percent lie. It shuts them up.

The fake news media can be defeated, but doing so requires that we refuse to be ignored. The truth is more powerful than fake news, but somebody has to tell it. The President stood up to fake news during the campaign, and won. He's standing up to it now. We're standing up to it on a daily basis. Together, we can win.

WHERE TO FIND REAL NEWS AND HONEST ANALYSIS

So if you can't trust the mainstream media, whom can you trust? How can you get real news? How can you equip yourself to bring about the next red wave if you can't separate fact from fiction, if you are being sold a bill of goods by the media establishment?

We are inundated on a daily basis with a whole lot of fake news, but we are also inundated with a tremendous amount of conservative opinion. How do we make sense of all of it?

There are times when the news is just the news. Unfortunately, those times seem to be limited to financial news and tragedy. While most major media outlets briefly keep us up-to-date on what has happened—rescue efforts, news about whether the terrorist or shooter has been neutralized, etc.—many outlets quickly pivot from news to opinion and even political debates surrounding the day's tragedy.

One aspect of my job on the *Jay Sekulow Live* radio broadcast is to break down the news for our audience, take live questions, and bring in experts when necessary to offer well-thought-out opinion.

We first report the facts, good or bad, because we want our audience to be educated on the issues and be able to share news about them with their friends and family. Then we break the facts down with analysis and opinion. We base our analysis on the knowledge we have gained individually over the years, research done leading up to the show, and reality.

Over the years, the show's impact has grown. We're now heard on over one thousand radio stations[35] each weekday, and we broadcast a television-quality, live video of our show on Facebook, Periscope, and the homepage of ACLJ.org. During traditional radio station breaks, we monitor breaking news and continue the discussion with the viewing audience while preparing to join our radio audience again once programming resumes.

Our show gives conservatives not only the straight-up news but also honest analysis and opinion. We take live callers during each show—some with questions, others with comments, includ-

ing those who completely disagree with our positions—to educate our listeners rather than only entertain them.

I believe there is a place for all kinds of conservative media,
yet I am especially proud of the team assembled for our broadcast and the transparency with which it is delivered—live. You
not only get the chance to hear our voices, but you can also see
us in the studio as the program unfolds in real time.

If you are looking for a place to get the news, receive analysis
from experts in their fields of law, policy, politics, and government affairs, I would encourage you—if you are not doing so
already—to become a regular listener or viewer of the *Jay Sekulow Live* broadcast.

My dad and I are no strangers to cable and network news. We
decide when to go on other shows and provide our honest analy-
ses about the topics we have agreed to discuss. There are great
shows, too many to list here, on which we appear regularly. Yet
it is great to have our own outlet to discuss the news you care
about, cut in with breaking news when appropriate, call out fake
news with fact-driven research, provide analysis with experts—all
while striving to be as accurate as possible in the 24/7 news cycle
we all live with today.

I am not suggesting that *Jay Sekulow Live* should be your only
source of news. Instead, use it as a check on what you see and
read being reported in the mainstream media. They have their
perspectives. We have our own.

On many issues, unlike regular media broadcasts, we also offer
you an opportunity to get involved—to take that next step in
civic engagement. We regularly invite and encourage that kind of
involvement on our show. Such grassroots actions include signing on to legal briefs filed in courts, as well as joining petitions
and letters delivered to Congress, the executive branch, international organizations, and leaders of other countries. As you have

read throughout this book, grassroots activism—like our constitutionally protected First Amendment right "to petition the Government for a redress of grievances"[36]—makes an undeniable and critically necessary impact.

I hope that, by reading this book, you are encouraged to become a regular participant on the *Jay Sekulow Live* broadcast. You will be informed of the news, educated with thoughtful analysis by practicing leaders in the field, and equipped to do battle with liberals on the key issues of the day.

Now you know how to spot fake news and where to find real news. But what do you do with that knowledge, and what is your responsibility to act on it?

In our final two chapters, we will detail just that.

CHAPTER 12

THE SACRED DUTY TO VOTE

THE RIGHT TO VOTE is one of the most precious rights our founders enshrined into our system of government.

You've seen the bumper sticker: "Don't Blame Me, I Voted for [fill in the blank with the name of the candidate who lost]." You may have heard it said, "You don't get to complain if you didn't vote." Our Founders called it, "No taxation without representation." The point is simple. Your vote is your voice. It's your way to impact the direction of your community, your state, and your nation.

It's your responsibility. It's your civic duty.

Many conservative Americans, even many Christians, may not fully understand the importance of voting. Some are just jaded.

DOES YOUR VOTE MATTER?

You are just one person. Candidate Trump got 61,201,031 votes in 2016.[1] How could yours possibly matter? In simplistic terms, by not voting, such an outlook becomes a self-fulfilling prophesy. If you don't vote, then your vote can't matter. If conservatives, evangelicals, and other Christians always voted, they would make up the most powerful voting bloc in the nation. The conservative principles we've long advocated would govern our society.

But, rather than spend time discussing bumper-sticker slogans about your vote mattering and esoteric philosophical concepts about the cumulative impact of voting, let's take a look at one recent example of how your vote can have major ramifications.

You've all heard how the 2000 election was decided for President Bush by only a few hundred votes in Florida—hanging chads and all. At the state level, the 2005 attorney general's election in Virginia was decided on election night in favor of Bob McDonnell by 323 votes (which grew to about a 360-vote advantage after a recount). Four years later, McDonnell was elected to the governorship by a margin of nearly 20 percentage points over the same person he had barely beaten in the race for attorney general. So Virginia's governorship in 2009 was greatly affected by just a few votes four years earlier.

But what about one vote? Does one vote really matter?

In fact, one single vote changed the makeup of one state's entire legislature in its last election. For the fourth time in history,[2] a state legislative race ended in a tie. Yes, a tie. In the 2017 election, Virginia's House of Delegates District 94 came down to 11,608 votes for each of the two candidates. After a recount and a court battle, the election officially ended in a tie. As is the case in a lot of states, the law required that the winner in tied elections be determined by the equivalent of the flip of a coin.

In this case, the board of elections put each of the candidates' names on a piece of paper, and put the two papers into two film canisters and then placed both canisters in a bowl. As representatives of the national media watched, and under the supervision of the other election board members, the canisters were swirled around and a board member picked one of them out at random. The candidate whose name was inside the canister that was selected became the delegate.

What made this situation even more intriguing was that the outcome of the race in the 94th House District determined whether the Republicans maintained control of the Virginia House of Delegates or whether Democrats would force a tie in the legislature and split control. It would determine the speaker of the House, the chairmanship of committees, the outcome of countless pieces of legislation, and whether that legislation ever reached the House floor or was killed in committee. It would affect the selection of judges and Supreme Court justices in Virginia.

The canister containing the name of the Republican, David Yancey, was drawn from the bowl, and the Virginia House of Delegates thereby remained under Republican control.

It came down to one vote. If one more person had shown up in one small legislative district (one of one hundred districts in Virginia), he or she could have changed two years' worth of legislation in Virginia. In fact, that vote might have determined the outcome of the Repeal Act—Virginia's version of the expansive abortion bill passed in New York we discussed earlier. In early 2019, this bill was defeated in committee in the Virginia House of Delegates[3]—a committee whose makeup had ultimately been impacted by Republican control in the House and decided by one vote in one election. The impact can be measured in countless ways. But it all came down to one person, one vote.

So yes, your vote does matter. It makes it even more stark when you realize that fewer than half of the registered voters in that Virginia district[4] voted.

That level of voter apathy is having a major impact not just in Virginia, but all over the country. You can bet that the majority of those who voted in that district, and almost everyone who didn't vote in that election, had no clue on Election Day how important their decision to vote—or not to vote—would prove to be.

The right to vote should be viewed through this lens in every election. It *does* matter, and it *will* have a massive impact.

But voting is more than our civic duty. As Christian Americans, voting is our sacred duty.

DON'T BURY YOUR VOTE

We are neither theologians nor preachers. We're just lawyers. But, as Christian lawyers, we need to consider the spiritual implications of our civic duty. It's probably not a sermon you've heard in church, but it should be.

In Romans 13, the Apostle Paul is direct. "Let every person be subject to the governing authorities," he says. "For there is no authority except from God, and those that exist have been instituted by God."[5] He goes on to say that government "is a minister of God to you for good."[6]

This is profound. But it's not something Christians think about a lot.

If God establishes systems of government, and government itself is a "minister of God," then how should that affect us as Christian citizens here in America?

We are incredibly blessed to live in a nation that allows us the freedom to select our leaders.

We don't live in Communist China, where the only "choice" is which Communist Party goon to vote for. We don't live in repressive Russia or in an Islamic theocracy like Iran, where dissent can mean death.

But we are blessed with more than the freedom to choose our leaders. "We the people" *are* the government in America.

We live in a democratic republic—a constitutional republic— where, as citizens, we select our leaders. We form the government. But only the "we" who get out and vote play a role in forming that government, selecting our leaders, and ensuring our voices are heard on the critical issues affecting our localities and our nation.

With this privilege comes a biblical imperative. As Paul concludes this passage on our spiritual civic duty, "For because of this you also pay taxes, for rulers are servants of God, devoting themselves to this very thing. Render to all what is due them: tax to whom tax is due; custom to whom custom; fear to whom fear; honor to whom honor."[7]

This means we have been given a role. We've not only been given the *ability* to select our leaders in America, we've been given the *responsibility* to do so wisely—something we will be held to account for one day.

Consider, for example, the Parable of the Talents in Matthew 25:14–30:

For it is just like a man about to go on a journey, who called his [servants] and entrusted his possessions to them. To one he gave five talents, to another, two, and to another, one, each according to his own ability; and he went on his journey. Immediately the one who had received the five talents went and traded with them, and gained five more talents. In the same manner the one who had received the two talents gained two more. But he who received the one talent went away, and dug a hole in the ground and hid his master's money.

· Now after a long time the master of those [servants] came and settled accounts with them. The one who had received the five talents came up and brought five more talents, saying, "Master, you entrusted five talents to me. See, I have gained five more talents." His master said to him, "Well done, good and faithful [servant]. You were faithful with a few things, I will put you in charge of many things; enter into the joy of your master."

Also the one who had received the two talents came up and said, "Master, you entrusted two talents to me. See, I have gained two more talents." His master said to him, "Well done, good and faithful [servant]. You were faithful with a few things, I will put you in charge of many things; enter into the joy of your master."

And the one also who had received the one talent came up and said, "Master, I knew you to be a hard man, reaping where you did not sow and gathering where you scattered no seed. And I was afraid, and went away and hid your talent in the ground. See, you have what is yours."

But his master answered and said to him, "You wicked, lazy [servant], you knew that I reap where I did not sow and gather where I scattered no seed. Then you ought to have put my money in the bank, and on my arrival I would have received my money back with interest. Therefore take away the talent from him, and give it to the one who has the ten talents."

For to everyone who has, more shall be given, and he will have an abundance; but from the one who does not have, even what he does have shall be taken away. Throw out the worthless [servant] into the outer darkness; in that place there will be weeping and gnashing of teeth.[8]

So here you have a story of three servants being entrusted with talents. They were each given responsibilities.

When the master returned and called them to account for what they did with the talents he gave them, he was very pleased with the first two servants because they took their responsibilities seriously, using their talents and reaping the benefits.

Yet the third servant, who had been given the one talent, had buried it in the ground and then returned it to the master without even trying.

He claimed he was too afraid because of how much he knew his master expected, but the Bible says he was in fact too "lazy" to do anything with what he'd been given—even calling him "wicked." The master was enraged because the servant did nothing with the blessing he received; he didn't even try. He buried his talent.

Like the servant, we've been given a blessing—the blessing of citizenship here in America. With that blessing of citizenship in a freedom-loving country comes a responsibility—voting.

Yet far too many Christians bury their vote, just like the wicked servant who buried his talent. They claim to be too afraid to get involved. Maybe the discourse is too appalling. Maybe the issues are just too complicated or uninteresting. Maybe the choices just don't seem to matter. Maybe the candidates are unsavory or don't perfectly represent our views.

But the real reason is that too many Christians are like the servant in the parable. They are just too lazy to care.

One day, we will all be held to account for this awesome responsibility we in America have been given. If we don't take this responsibility seriously, we will all live in a place where "there will be weeping and gnashing of teeth."

So don't bury your vote.

As Proverbs 29:2 says, "When the righteous increase, the people rejoice, but when the wicked rule, the people groan."[9]

This is really nothing new. We complain. We hear grumbling in our churches about the trajectory of our moral decay as a nation. Yet what is the Church doing about it? What are we doing about it?

We have the opportunity to be that change. We can—and *must*—take this responsibility seriously.

In Deuteronomy 1:13, God told the people of Israel, "Choose for your tribes wise, understanding, and experienced men, and I will appoint them as your heads."[10] It is no different today. We need to take the time to find out about the qualities and qualifications of those who are running for office. We need to encourage good men and women to seek public office.

Politics has become so unsavory—so corrupted by lies and scandals—that many Christians have just abandoned the public arena. This vacuum is then filled by everything that we disagree with—and so, yes, our choices become repugnant. But it's a problem of our own doing. And we can start to solve it by engaging in the political system again—by voting.

Bear in mind that this problem goes far beyond the elections most people even think about: the presidential and congressional elections.

Are our schools a mess? When was the last time you paid attention to a school board election?

Are our churches being limited in what they can do? When was the last time you paid attention to your local zoning board or county board of supervisors?

The next elections are just around the corner. Do you know who is running, what they stand for, or even who your current elected officials are?

As Christians blessed to live in America, we are responsible for doing far more than just showing up at the polls on Election Day.

We can't just vote. Like providing for our families, training our children, or any other biblical imperative, voting requires thought and foresight.

Find out who your elected officials or candidates for office are. Pick up the phone and call their offices. Try to meet them. Find out where they stand on the issues. And pray.

As Paul told Timothy, "First of all, then, I urge that supplications, prayers, intercessions, and thanksgivings be made for all people, for kings and all who are in high positions, that we may lead a peaceful and quiet life, godly and dignified in every way."[11]

Some would disagree. They fear selecting the wrong leader or letting politics consume them. Some say, "But our citizenship is in heaven"[12] (Philippians 3:20), "Give back to Caesar what is Caesar's and to God what is God's"[13] (Mark 12:17), "We are to be in the world but not of it"[14] (loosely translated from John 17:14–15), and "[T]hose in positions of authority have been placed there by God"[15] (Romans 13:1).

All of this is true. But remember that God has specifically ordained government. And that system of government under which we live is a representative form of government. So if that system is established by God, then we have a role to play in it. Christ said to give unto Caesar that which is Caesar's. In America, **we get to choose who "Caesar" is**. The Jews to whom he spoke had no such choice. Shame on us if we take ours for granted.

Now, it is very important to remember what Scripture says in Psalm 146:3, "Put not your trust in princes, in a son of man, in whom there is no salvation."[16]

We cannot put our trust in politicians. News Flash: They will fail us time and time again.

Remember the greatest leader Israel ever had—"a man after God's own heart."[17] David had a man killed, was an adulterer, and his kids were literally a royal mess. Yet God used him in spite of all of this.

So even though our political options may sometimes fall short of what we would like to see in our leaders, we can't use that as an excuse to sit on the sidelines waiting for the perfect David to come along, because even he won't be.

We cannot allow politics to influence our faith. But we *must* act out our faith by influencing and participating in our government.

The fact remains, voting is a spiritual exercise. Our Founding Fathers established our nation on this principle.

Yet our secular, humanist, postmodern society has rejected this principle—putting up a wall of separation between church and state, a phrase that the Constitution does not include. It was paraphrased from Thomas Jefferson, who wrote a letter in 1802 to the Danbury Baptist Association asserting that the new American government would never interfere with or attempt to control the Church. It was never intended to prevent the Church from following its moral duty and influencing our government.

But not only has our fallen culture shunned the sacred nature of electing our leaders, the Church has forsaken it as well. The Church has bought into this lie hook, line, and sinker.

WHERE IS THE CHURCH?

When was the last time you heard a sermon on an overtly political topic? When was the last time the Church engaged in a political debate?

What about the lives of unborn babies that are being snuffed out on a daily basis?

What about the plague of jihadist genocide growing worldwide?

What about the secular indoctrination of our children in the education system?

What about an entitlement culture that says, "if anyone is not willing to work," then we should make someone else pay for it?[18]

What about angry atheists who are seeking to wipe away any vestige of our Christian heritage as a nation—from our national motto "In God We Trust" on our currency to "under God" in our Pledge of Allegiance?

We fear the Church in America has largely grown soft. It is not leading.

How can Christians be expected to take seriously their sacred duty to vote—since we the people are the government—if our pulpits are pathetically silent and timid?

In America, the land of the free, we've been given the blessing of self-governance. We've been given the five talents.

If we as people of faith fail to exercise our right to vote—the responsibility that comes with the blessing of freedom—we will have wasted it.

We will have buried our talent in the ground. And, as occurred in the parable, we may have it taken away.

But our responsibilities go beyond the simple act of voting.

That is only a start.

It's "self" governance. It's us. Governance is our direct responsibility.

That means that Christians and the Church as a whole must be willing to speak out on specific issues.

We know many churches are leery about speaking out on

certain issues because they don't want to lose their tax-exempt status.

We understand that this is not wholly the fault of the Church. The law has been intentionally contorted and misconstrued by the Left to dissuade Christian conservatives from speaking out in their churches.

A law called the Johnson Amendment prevents churches from engaging in overt political campaigning, but there is nothing preventing churches from speaking out on specific issues.

There is an effort on the Left to confuse and distort the truth about the Johnson Amendment in order to silence the Church.

At the ACLJ, we're working to try to repeal the Johnson Amendment, and President Trump has issued an executive order that says that the Johnson Amendment should be construed narrowly so as to limit its damage. We are working on a permanent legislative fix to this issue as well, something that may very much depend on the outcome of the next elections.

But let us be crystal clear: there is *nothing* preventing the Church from speaking out on the issues that matter most.

The Johnson Amendment prevents charities and churches from endorsing or opposing specific political candidates for office, but it does *not* limit the right of churches to talk about issues. It does *not* mean that pastors should be afraid to promote biblical principles in public policy or to preach about specific issues.

The Church must stop being silent.

WE'RE RESPONSIBLE TO HOLD OUR LEADERS ACCOUNTABLE

We must be willing to call our members of the U.S. Congress and demand they vote to stop forcing us to subsidize Planned

Parenthood—an abortion behemoth that slaughters hundreds of thousands of innocent lives each year.

We must be willing to attend and speak up during county board meetings when they are considering resolutions that would limit the number of people who can attend Bible studies in private homes.[19]

We must make our voices heard at school board meetings when they are considering forcing homeschooled children to endure a grand inquisition for their faith, requiring them to answer questions about their religious beliefs.[20]

We must engage the educational system and participate in Parent Teacher Association meetings when children in public schools are being forced to participate in Buddhist-based meditation programs.[21]

Each of these outrages has occurred. Each is an issue that we at the ACLJ have been fighting. But where is the Church?

In the first situation cited above, a county was going to ban groups of a certain size from meeting in private homes if they were planning to do so on a weekly basis. This vote would likely have slipped by unnoticed had not we, along with some other concerned citizens, spoken out. As Matthew Clark (a coauthor of this book) wrote in an op-ed in the *Washington Examiner*:[22]

This proposed "Group Assembly in Residential Dwellings" zoning ordinance amendment not only poses a grave and fundamental violation of the U.S. Constitution but smacks of the worst type of government overreach....

I never imagined hosting a Bible study in my home could one day be a violation of the law, but that's exactly what this proposal could do.

On a recent Wednesday night, I joined dozens of other

concerned residents of the county at one of three planned Fairfax County Board of Supervisors' community meetings to voice our outrage about this proposal.

I explained how the proposed amendment would violate the right to free speech, the right to religious expression, and the right to freedom of assembly.

The Supreme Court has specifically held that it would be a direct violation of the Constitution for an ordinance "to make criminal the exercise of the right of assembly simply because its exercise may be 'annoying' to some people."

That's precisely what the proposed ordinance aims to do.

It limits the rights of... Fairfax residents to peaceably assemble in their own homes, to hold Bible studies there, and conduct many other lawful activities.

It not only violates the U.S. Constitution, it violates Virginia's religious freedom [statute] by substantially burdening an individual's religious right to hold a Bible study in their own home if it exceeds a certain number of participants.

In fact, the explanation for this proposal on Fairfax County's website specifically denotes "religious meetings" as one of the intended targets of this ordinance.

Thankfully, by standing up and fighting back, we defeated the proposal. As Clark explained at the time:[23]

This is a clear sign that county officials got the message loud and clear: You cannot attack free speech, the right to assembly, and religious liberty and get away with it.

The Constitution won the day in this instance, but only because people were willing to speak out....

The fact that I first learned of the proposal the same day that I was to begin hosting a Bible study in my own home made this particularly concerning to me. The blatant targeting of religious liberty and freedom of assembly was shocking.

Imagine what could have happened if people hadn't shown up at that board meeting. How much harder would it have been to undo this ordinance once it was passed? And how many Bible study groups would have been squelched? How many other counties in other states would have tried the same draconian tactics?

It's not enough to just vote; speaking out makes the difference.

In the second example, a local school board in Virginia had instituted a regulation to undermine the state's homeschooling laws by forcing children to defend their faith before the school board in order to be homeschooled.

The local school board policy required fourteen-year-old children to stand before the school board and submit to interrogation about their religious beliefs.

As we wrote at the time:[24]

[It was] aimed at homeschool families that fall under Virginia's decades-old religious exemption statute, which acknowledges parents' rights to direct the upbringing and education of their children.

The longstanding state statute allows parents to homeschool their children without reporting to the state if they have an objection to attending school outside the home that is based on "bona fide religious training or belief."

The Goochland school board decided that not only do parents have to submit the basis for their religious beliefs for choosing to homeschool their children, but that it could require children, minors, between the ages of 14 and 18 to appear before the school board and undergo an inquisition about their own independent basis for their religious beliefs....

To be clear this policy has no basis in Virginia law. In fact the policy directly violates Virginia's religious freedom statutes and the U.S. Constitution....

The school board took a very simple statute that protects religious freedom (in fact Virginia has some of the best home-school and religious liberty statutes in the country) and turned it on its head, claiming confusion and a need to impose draconian requirements on parents and their minor children.

No child (and that's what a 14 year old is) should ever be forced to stand before a government body to give account for their faith. It is an unbelievable abuse of power and violation of human rights to think that a school board could force a child to essentially testify about his or her religious beliefs and undercuts the very purpose for which Virginia's religious exemption statute was enacted.

This is not the first school board, nor will it be the last, to assert that it has the power to determine how parents should raise their children.

It may be harder to repeal these onerous attacks than it is to block them in the first place, but it can be done, as we did in this situation through an aggressive legal-advocacy campaign.

But it's just another example of why voting matters, and why, after leaving the ballot box, paying attention matters. When we speak out, we can effect major change.

But it's more than just local politics, we can effect global change.

Over the last decade or so, up to 90 percent of Iraq's Christian population has been decimated.[25] Two-thirds of Syria's Christians have been forced to flee or be slaughtered.[26]

Christians have been crucified and beheaded for refusing to renounce Christ. Dozens were massacred in church bombings on Palm Sunday 2017 in Egypt.[27] Hundreds were slaughtered on Easter Sunday 2019 in Sri Lanka.[28] Dozens more have been slaughtered in the Philippines[29] and elsewhere.

All-out genocide is being waged against Christians in the Middle East. Again, where is the Church? We must do more.

In Romans 13:4, the Apostle Paul makes clear God's view of government's role in this situation, "But if you do what is evil, be afraid; for [the government] does not bear the sword for nothing; for it is a minister of God, an avenger who brings wrath on the one who practices evil."[30]

It is up to us as Christian citizens—as the Church—to spur our government, "We the people," into action.

It is important to remember that our responsibility is not affected by whether our candidate wins. Our responsibility doesn't end after the election. We still have a duty as citizens to make our voices heard.

As we explained in chapter nine, we at the ACLJ advocated during the Obama administration for the U.S. government to officially recognize that the atrocities being waged by ISIS against Christians in the Middle East were "genocide." The Obama administration was reluctant to take even this simple step.

So, exercising our First Amendment rights, we petitioned the government for a redress of grievances. After obtaining hundreds of thousands of signatures, we sent numerous legal letters to the administration, and conducted a massive media advocacy campaign. And in early 2016, the Obama administration relented and officially recognized that there was in fact a "genocide against . . . Christians."[31]

As we previously detailed, we're working with the Trump administration and pressuring the United Nations to take action and protect the victims of genocide seeking to return to their homelands.

But again, where is the Church? Imagine what could be accomplished if millions of American Christians joined with millions more around the globe to defend persecuted Christians.

We must take that "talent," that blessing, that responsibility, and use it. We must not bury our vote.

WHAT'S AT STAKE

So, with the next elections looming, what's at stake?

The 2020 presidential election could drastically affect the direction of our nation: whether taxpayer funding for abortion is expanded, whether Israel is betrayed, whether life is protected, whether religious liberty is respected, federal regulations, judges, the Supreme Court, and so much more. It all turns on whether President Trump is reelected.

The congressional elections could determine major legislative priorities. With control of the Senate on the line, the record pace of federal judicial appointments hangs in the balance. The change of just a few Senate seats could end the confirmation of conservative judges. Imagine what might happen if another vacancy opens on the already closely divided Supreme Court. The party in control of the Senate could change the course of every law in the country for decades.

These elections could also have a massive impact on whether the American people are going to be forced to continue to pay for nearly half of the billion-dollar annual budget of the biggest abortion business in America. After Planned Parenthood was exposed for selling the body parts of babies they had aborted to pad their bottom line, earning record profits, and reportedly landing themselves under a federal Justice Department investigation,[32] Congress failed to defund them. The House voted to defund Planned Parenthood, but the Senate fell one vote short in its failed effort to repeal Obamacare. Now; with the Nancy Pelosi–led Democrats in control of the House of Representatives, any further attempt to defund the abortion giant will depend greatly on the outcome of the next elections.

In addition, several other pro-life bills could be affected greatly by the next elections, including the Pain-Capable Unborn Child Protection Act (the twenty-week abortion ban).

Several other key pieces of legislation also teeter on the edge of passage. The Johnson Amendment discussed earlier, which unfairly censors churches, could finally be repealed. The tax reform measures that were passed at the end of 2017 are not permanent. If Democrats maintain control of the House and take control of the Senate, they could repeal them and raise your taxes again. The full repeal of Obamacare cannot happen unless Republicans retain control of the Senate and take back the House.

And none of this will be possible unless President Trump is re-elected.

The next Congress could decide critical issues regarding our out-of-control spending, military readiness, and other budgetary issues. The outcome of the immigration debate and border security hangs in the balance.

There are other key issues that are not often considered when it comes to the control of Congress. The next elections will determine if we will be forced to endure more time with Speaker Pelosi, are faced with a Senate Majority Leader Chuck Schumer, and are subjected to Democrat control of key committee chairmanships in both chambers. Imagine Democrats controlling *all* of the investigations into the out-of-control bureaucracy, the abuse of the DOJ and FBI, and any number of other key concerns.

A continued Democrat House, a Democrat-controlled Senate, and any one of a few dozen Democrat wannabe nominees as president would lead to the dismantling, during their first one hundred days in power, of every victory we've won in the last several years. It's not far-fetched. It's not hyperbole. It's already been promised.

The only way to stop this is to bring about the next red wave.

With this much at stake, you cannot afford to bury your vote.

CHAPTER 13

REDRESS OF GRIEVANCES

SO YOU HAVE YOUR VOICE. You have your vote. You are ready to refuse to be ignored. How do you turn that into actual action? How do you turn that passion and willingness to act into the next red wave?

The story of the IRS targeting scandal is both a cautionary tale of government corruption and a road map for future victory. The Tea Party brought about the last red wave—a red wave that Donald Trump tapped back into to win the presidency in 2016.

The lessons we have learned from the Tea Party and the IRS targeting scandal—which marked the first time the American people saw the Deep State's subversion for what it was—provide us with an invaluable playbook for the next red wave.

Just look how important the Tea Party was. It wasn't a political party. Not a single candidate for elected office ran on the Tea Party ticket. There was no Tea Party ticket. Yet it made a lasting impact. Why? Because it was a grassroots uprising of the people.

But if it was snuffed out in its infancy and suffocated by the IRS, how do we know it was so powerful and important? **Because the Left wanted to shut it down.**

President Obama railed against the Tea Party. It wasn't so

much a dog whistle as directly pointing the finger. In 2010, he warned, "Right now all around this country there are groups with harmless-sounding names...." He endlessly attacked them, fearmongering that he wanted to make "sure that foreign companies can't influence our elections."[1]

Sound familiar? Somehow, when conservatives activate and go to the polls, the Left goes back to the same tired refrain about some foreign attempt to influence our elections. That's what the Left thinks of you—conservatives who want to ensure that the Constitution is followed as the founders of our great nation intended are some kind of foreign entity posing a danger to our country.

The Left is cunning. It doesn't bother attacking something if doing so won't advance its cause or if it is something that it doesn't fear. Yes, the Left tried to paint the Tea Party as the dark money that it constantly fearmongers about. But the reality is, the Left feared the Tea Party because the Tea Party activated a group of people who had never before been active in politics.

The Left foresaw just how powerful this group of people could be. The Left and the Deep State tried to suppress them, and they almost succeeded.

But candidate Trump reactivated these same people and went on to win the White House.

The Tea Party was a collection of moms and dads, history teachers and construction workers, college-educated conservatives and street-smart graduates of the school of hard knocks. They didn't regularly donate to political campaigns. They didn't typically run for office. They were not political elites. They were just regular Americans. They cared about the direction our nation was going, and they were tired of losing.

Most of the time in previous years, they probably voted, but they were not politically active. That all changed in 2010 and then again in 2016. This was a new segment of the conservative electorate that was not only fired up, but also organized. They were ready for battle. They were ready to go toe-to-toe with the radicals of leftist academia. They were ready to take on the extremists of MoveOn and Occupy Wall Street.

In fact, they were just as ready to take on the Republican establishment. This made them even more dangerous, because the Tea Party was pushing RINOs (Republicans In Name Only) back toward the Right. Those squishes who could once be counted on to give in to the demands of the Left were now—if for no other reason than their own sense of political self-preservation—moving back to the Right.

The Tea Party was a force to be reckoned with. It was a threat to the liberal elites. Thus, it had to be stopped. The Deep State did the dirty work.

The Left almost got away with it. It almost buried the most effective catalyst of conservative change that we had seen in years. But it didn't, and the founding organizing principles of the Tea Party might just hold the key to taking back America with a new grassroots movement.

We're not suggesting that we need a Tea Party 2.0. The name doesn't matter. It doesn't have to be an exact replication of the Tea Party, but a replication of what made the Tea Party. It *is* the next red wave.

It was just people like you and me. It was people who cared about conservative principles. It was people who wanted, for lack of a better phrase, to make America great again. It was people who were willing to fight for what they believed in. It was people who were tired of losing, tired of being relegated to the sidelines, tired of seeing all that they, their parents, and their grandparents had worked so hard for be eroded away.

The Tea Party taught us that if you fight back hard enough,

you can defeat the Deep State. It also taught us that individual Americans, when engaging in the kind of civic involvement the Constitution envisioned, can make a massive impact.

Take, for example, the First Amendment. If we were to ask what the First Amendment says, most Americans could probably identify the freedoms of speech, religion, and the press that it safeguards. Most would recognize the immortal phrase "Congress shall make no law respecting an establishment of religion, or prohibiting the free exercise thereof; or abridging the freedom of speech, or of the press."[2] But that's not the end of the First Amendment.

The end of the First Amendment, though far lesser known, is just as important, if not more so.

Yes, freedom of speech and religion and the press are vitally important. But what comes next can instruct us as we seek the next red wave. Here's how it ends in context. "Congress shall make no law...abridging...the right of the people peaceably to *assemble, and to petition* the Government for a redress of grievances."[3]

That is the key. It's what the Tea Party did. And it is exactly what we need to do today.

It is the right to gather with like-minded individuals and take a stand for what you believe is right. It's the right to demand that your government—including the Deep State bureaucracy—be held accountable to you.

And while you have probably heard of the right of assembly, the final clause is even lesser known, but just as powerful. The right to "petition the government for a redress of grievances"[4] is near and dear to our hearts at the ACLJ. It's what we do each and every day.

If you go to ACLJ.org, you will find dozens upon dozens of petitions signed by millions of Americans. We use each one of these petitions in our advocacy on an array of issues. Yes, one was to end the IRS abuse.[5] We repeatedly took that petition to members of Congress as we showed them individuals in their districts who didn't want them to give up the fight against the IRS—people who demanded they hold the IRS accountable. It was this, in turn, that helped keep the congressional investigations alive. We were then able to use information gleaned from these investigations in federal court as evidence to eventually win the case.

But it all started with individuals like you who were willing to stand up and be heard, to make a difference—to "petition the government for a redress of grievances."[6]

We've taken these petitions to Congress; we've used them to sign our amicus (friend-of-the-court) briefs at the Supreme Court; and we've taken them to world leaders to help secure the release of imprisoned pastors.

Petitions really do have power, and they are right there, enumerated as a constitutionally protected right of the people in the First Amendment.

But it takes individuals like you being willing to sign, being willing to donate, and being willing to give of your time to gather with others of like mind to make an impact.

This was the playbook of the Tea Party. And it is the road map of the next red wave. **Gather. Grow. Go.** (You may have heard something like this from your church or place of worship, but the point is simple and applies outside the church, too.)

GATHER

First, like-minded people who want to change America for the better must be willing to gather together. It could be through social media, Facebook groups, and meetings at your local library.

But gathering is the first step. Until we gather, we are islands unto ourselves. Yet when we combine, we are able to unify our efforts and synthesize our messages. There truly is strength in numbers.

Think about it: the Left always complains about "special interest" groups in politics. Usually, the Left goes to war against "big oil" or "big pharma" special interests. The point is, these "special interests" work because they represent a lot of people. The National Rifle Association (NRA) doesn't hold massive power in Washington just because it has a few million dollars to throw around. It holds sway because it has millions and millions of members—members who are incredibly engaged. Members of Congress know that if they vote the wrong way on the Second Amendment, they are going to lose more than dollars; they are going to lose thousands upon thousands of votes. That matters. That makes an impact.

Likewise, the Left capitulates to Planned Parenthood with every vote because Planned Parenthood and the abortion industry's special interests will not allow a single Democrat to vote pro-life or even make a single neutral comment on life. Each year, Planned Parenthood not only takes hundreds of millions of our tax dollars, but it also then directly funds liberal, pro-abortion candidates through its PAC, the Planned Parenthood Action Fund. Planned Parenthood uses this immense influence to shape pro-abortion policy at the local, state, and federal levels—in the courts, in Congress, and in the court of public opinion.

So what if you were a "special interest"? What if you, your friends, and your neighbors could wield that kind of political power?

Our point is: *you absolutely can.*

GROW

Gathering may be the first step, and the Tea Party did it well, but growing is where you take a group and turn it into a movement. This is where the Left struck at the Tea Party. They knew that the explosive growth of the Tea Party was going to make it a major player. So, when the Tea Party began to grow, the IRS Deep State went right for the jugular. It cut off the Tea Party's oxygen. It took away its ability to raise money.

Think about it. Hundreds of groups were springing up across America. They were loosely affiliated, at best. They had common conservative goals, but at the beginning they weren't connected to each other. They were a true grassroots movement. So when hundreds of these groups began springing up, the Left got scared.

How could it stop a movement like this? There was no individual leader; there was no CEO or president of the Tea Party whom it could target. The Tea Party movement comprised individual, unconnected groups of anywhere from a half dozen to thousands of members.

We know that the IRS targeted nearly five hundred[7] of these groups, which means that there were an average of about ten conservative groups in every state. So how in the world could the Left possibly combat this? No single leader to target; no parent organization to tear down; no political figurehead against whom to run negative opposition-research ads. Other than a general conservative agenda tying them together, these groups had only one thing in common.

They had all applied for tax-exempt status—some as 501(c)(3) charitable, educational, and public interest groups and some as 501(c)(4) social welfare groups.

By targeting the tax-exempt status of these groups, the IRS Deep State and the Left went after their ability to raise funds.

Not only did the IRS make it nearly impossible for them to raise money—because the Tea Party's tax-exempt status was in IRS purgatory—but it also stained the Tea Party's name, corrupting its appeal to potential donors.

Imagine, all those groups being held up by the IRS. They must be bad, right? Bad people—tax cheats—are held up by the IRS. You wouldn't want to be associated with people being investigated by the IRS, right? In fact, if these groups were being forced to send their membership rolls to the IRS, then the IRS would know you were in the group, and the IRS might come after you. I bet you don't want to be in that group anymore.

In the law, this is known as a "chilling" effect. It's something that stops you from taking a legal action or exercising a right by making it hard to do. That's exactly what the IRS did to the Tea Party. And it shows the importance of growing as a movement.

It is through growth, whether it is membership or financial, that a group becomes a movement—a force to be reckoned with.

As the Tea Party grew, it began to have influence. It became a household name. It made headlines. It got Googled. It was a snowball effect.

As more disenchanted, everyday, conservative Americans learned about the Tea Party as a concept, they began starting their own groups in their own, local communities. What had started as a few dozen conservatives in a few dozen community groups exploded exponentially into arguably the largest grass-roots political movement in modern history.

As the movement grew, passionate individuals were able to coalesce around a common set of goals—conservative principles—and their power grew.

But the movement didn't stop at gathering and growing; it turned that impassioned, organized movement into action.

In order to replicate the kind of impact the Tea Party had,

conservatives must once again not only gather together around a common set of principles, but they must also be willing to put their time, energy, and money where their mouths are. That's exactly what the Tea Party did, and if we do it again, we can bring about the next red wave.

GO

The last thing the Tea Party did was to get involved. It not only met and raised money, but it also actively engaged in the political and policy debates that were shaping America. It didn't just say, "Boy, taxes are high. That's too bad." It didn't just gather with friends to talk about how much its members didn't like high taxes. They showed up at political rallies and town halls. They directly asked their members of Congress how they were going to vote. And they went to the ballot box. The Tea Party voted in droves.

The Tea Party sent a wave of new senators and representatives to the Capitol. It took over town councils and school boards. Some Tea Party members ran for office, but more often they found someone who they believed could get the job done and threw their full support behind that person. The Tea Party members mobilized so effectively that they were able to take down House majority leader Eric Cantor (R-VA). Congressional leaders don't often lose in the general election, and they very rarely lose their primaries. Cantor had been on the cusp of becoming House speaker. Yet, in the 2014 election, before Speaker John Boehner retired, Cantor lost.

As an aside, we enjoyed working with Leader Cantor on many issues important to the ACLJ and our members. He is a good man and has been missed on Capitol Hill. Unfortunately, his campaign staff waited way too long to calculate the power of the Tea Party in his primary.

How did he lose? It wasn't a scandal. It wasn't some singular vote on a bill. He just got beat by a candidate behind whom the Tea Party had rallied. The Tea Party simply mobilized. Its members acted. How did he lose? By failing to embrace the Tea Party.

A similar course of events led to the election of President Donald Trump in 2016. It wasn't the Tea Party per se, but it was a similar, *much larger* uprising composed of everyday Americans who said enough is enough. Washington is broken. It's time to drain the swamp. And, for the first time in American history, the American people sent to the White House a man who hadn't held any government office.

That is the kind of impact that you can have.

That is the kind of power you do have.

But you have to go. The fact that you picked up this book means that you care. You have the passion. You want the next red wave. You expect more from your politicians than you are getting. You are sick of losing. You are sick of failure. You are tired of seeing the American dream eroded away—one political lie, one careless vote, one political smear, one unconscionable betrayal after another.

You truly care about the future of our nation. But you may often feel alone, helpless, and powerless. It doesn't have to be that way. You can win again. You can silence the critics. You can restore the American dream.

When you **gather**, you will not feel alone. You will see that dozens in your community, thousands in your state, and millions in your country want the same America you do. When you **grow**, you will not feel helpless. You will feel empowered to effectuate real change. And when you **go**, you will see results. You will see the impact of a revolution you started. You will achieve the next red wave.

Conservatives must once again unite. We must go to the polls. We must go to county and city council meetings, school board meetings, party precinct meetings, local political events, town halls, primaries, and conventions.

Most local political races and candidates are organized and decided in small, smoke-filled rooms because so few people show up that they are able to exert an influence far out of proportion to their numbers. It doesn't have to be that way.

We can pick the best politicians because we attended local meetings and know who these people are and that they will represent our interests on the town council or in Congress. We can ensure our candidates make it onto the ballot by organizing petition drives. We can make sure our issues become the center of the political campaign by organizing, donating, and speaking out. We can ensure that our voices are heard in Washington by turning out to the polls and making sure our friends, neighbors, coworkers, and fellow members of our places of worship understand the issues, know the candidates, and vote their consciences, too.

By following the model of the Tea Party—especially now that the IRS has been "bludgeoned" and put in its place—we can reshape the political landscape. That's how the Tea Party shocked the political elites in 2010. It's how President Trump won in 2016. And it's how we can finally get the change we deserve in Washington in 2020 and beyond.

That's what we hope this book contributes to. Thousands and thousands of normal Americans who are willing to take a stand for what they believe in. When you stand together with thousands of other like-minded Americans, you can—and will—accomplish great feats. Together, we took down the out-of-control IRS that sought to silence conservatives, and together we can take down the Deep State and the radical Left.

We can take back our republic. Our impact will start as a group effort. It will grow into a movement. The IRS can't stop it. The Deep State can't slow it down. The Left can't defeat it.

But it's up to you to start it. It's how you will bring about the next red wave.

ACKNOWLEDGMENTS

I can say with certainty that this book—a comprehensive grass-roots guide for conservative victory with detailed examples of the opposing forces we face in elections—would have been almost impossible to complete at the standard I required without the invaluable contributions of my coauthors Benjamin Sisney and Matthew Clark. This book would not exist without the encouragement of my agent, Curtis Wallace, to write this book while serving as a guide throughout the entire process from beginning to publication. I would like to thank Aaron Hodges and the graphics team at Regency Productions for working tirelessly on a truly excellent cover—the first thing people see at the bookstore, in television interviews promoting the book, and even when ordering the book online. Thank you to my dad, Jay Sekulow, for writing the foreword and Sean Hannity for so enthusiastically endorsing my first book as main author. Finally, I must thank Anna Sekulow, my wife, for her support and insight throughout my first major writing endeavor.

Yet there would be no book without the team at Hachette/Center Street. Rolf Zettersten, my publisher, championed this project from the start. Kate Hartson, editorial director, made sure to keep us on track and provided valuable guidance and suggestions as we started and ultimately completed the book. It has been exciting to work with Patsy Jones, vice president of marketing, and Billy Clark, vice president of sales, to ensure *The Next Red Wave* reaches as many readers as possible. The entire editorial and production teams at Hachette/Center Street also deserve acknowledgment as they assisted my coauthors and me in writing the best possible book that we were capable of producing.

While *The Next Red Wave* certainly focuses on the upcoming elections in 2020, I believe it will impact the country for decades to come. This is a guidebook for conservatives that can be utilized in future elections at the local, state, and national levels. I wrote *The Next Red Wave* with my coauthors after the knowledge we have collectively gained over years of political campaign experience and our work as attorneys at the American Center for Law and Justice (ACLJ), where law, policy, and politics often overlap. I know you were encouraged to take your political engagement to the next level after reading *The Next Red Wave*, and hope you will ask like-minded conservatives to purchase the book so that we are fully prepared for victory in 2020 and beyond. It is time for *The Next Red Wave*.

NOTES

FOREWORD

1   *Board of Airport Commissioners v. Jews for Jesus*, 482 U.S. 569 (1987).

2   *See, e.g.*, https://aclj.org/government-corruption/aclj-government-accountability-project-issues-foia-report-to-congress-exposing-deep-state-government-corruption; https://aclj.org/foia.

1. PREPARING FOR THE NEXT RED WAVE—WINDS ARE FORMING

1   The author of this book, Jordan Sekulow, and the coauthors, Benjamin Sisney and Matthew Clark, have been working and collaborating together for more than a decade. References to "we" in this book refer to stories or projects worked on by all or more than one of them. Specific references to "I" mainly refer directly to Jordan Sekulow.

2. ELECTIONS HAVE CONSEQUENCES

1   *See, e.g.,* "Pr. William Co. Greenlights Nokesville Mosque after Year of Debate," WTOP, https://wtop.com/prince-william-county/2017/06/pr-william-co-greenlights-nokesville-mosque-after-years-of-debate/ ("the mosque would violate county policy by accessing a county sewer line").

2   One example is RLUIPA, the Religious Land Use and Institutionalized Persons Act of 2000, 42 U.S.C. §§ 2000cc. This law protects religious institutions and churches from unwarranted zoning discrimination. But even with strong federal statutes like this, we still have to battle localities that will do anything for the almighty dollar to zone (non-tax-paying) churches right out of town. The law in this area is far more complex than it needs to be, but it is one area in which we have had—and can continue to have—tremendous success in the courts. But as we explain in further chapters, it takes you standing up for your rights to do so.

3   We say artificial minimum wage because wages in a free economy must be based on skill and supply and demand. A one-size-fits-all wage set by politicians in Washington or the statehouse is the epitome of artificial. Why any politician thinks a teenage kid working a paper route or flipping burgers deserves to make the same as a mature, experienced father or mother of three is beyond us. The reality is if you have $15 an hour and you need two positions filled, you could pay the kid $5 an hour for menial tasks and the more experienced person $10. A minimum wage means you are forced to pay them both $7.50 an hour. And if the Left gets their way with a $15 minimum wage, you're forced to lay one of them off, and can't get the work done.

4   The DACA (Deferred Action for Childhood Arrivals) program began in June of 2012 and provided that "certain people who came to the United States as children and meet several guidelines may request consideration of deferred action for a period of two years, subject to renewal. They are also eligible for work authorization. Deferred action is a use of prosecutorial discretion to defer removal action against an individual for a certain period of time. Deferred

action does not provide lawful status." https://www.uscis.gov/archive/consideration-deferred-action-childhood-arrivals-daca.

3. WE COULD LOSE

1 https://www.foxbusiness.com/politics/key-democrats-say-they-want to-impeach-kavanaugh-can-they.

2 While the origin of this saying is unknown, it is consistently borne out by the data. *See, e.g.,* "Americans Down on Congress, OK with own Representative," Gallup, http://news.gallup.com/poll/162362/americans-down-congress-own-representative.aspx; "Congress has 11% approval ratings but 96% incumbent reelection rate, meme says," Politifact, http://www.politifact.com/truth-o-meter/statements/2014/nov/11/facebook-posts/congress-has-11-approval-ratings-96-incumbent-re-e/.

3 Scott Horsly, "Obama Campaigns for 16th Time in Nevada," NPR, September 18, 2008, https://www.npr.org/templates/story/story.php?storyId=94748535.

4 See *Board of Airport Commissioners v. Jews for Jesus,* 482 U.S. 569 (1987); *Board of Education v. Mergens,* 496 U.S. 226 (1990); *Bray v. Alexandria Women's Health Clinic,* 506 U.S. 263 (1993); *Lamb's Chapel v. Center Moriches School District,* 508 U.S. 384 (1993); *Schenck v. Pro-Choice Network of W.N.Y.,* 519 U.S. 357 (1997); *Operation Rescue v. National Organization for Women, consolidated as Scheidler v. National Organization for Women, Inc., 537 U.S. 393 (2003)*; *McConnell v. FEC,* 540 U.S. 93 (2003) (unanimously vindicating political contributions of minors as constitutionally protected free speech); *Pleasant Grove v. Summum,* 555 U.S. 460 (2009).

5 http://nymag.com/intelligencer/2018/08/republicans-beginning-to-abandon-doomed-house-candidates.html.

6 https://www.cnbc.com/2018/10/31/nancy-pelosi-is-confident-democrats-will-gain-30-seats-flip-the-house.html.

7 Donna Brazile, *Hacks: The Inside Story of the Break-ins and Breakdowns That Put Donald Trump in the White House* (New York:

Hachette Books, 2017), https://www.amazon.com/Hacks-Inside-Break-ins-Breakdowns-Donald/dp/0316478504/ref=asc_df_03164 78504.

4. THE DEEP STATE RISES

1   https://www.washingtontimes.com/news/2017/jul/6/donald-trump target-of-leaks-at-rate-of-one-a-day/.
2   http://www.hsgac.senate.gov/download/state-secrets-how-an-ava lanche-of-media-leaks-is-harming-national-security.
3   Ibid.
4   https://www.cnn.com/2017/06/08/politics/james-comey-testimony-donald-trump/index.html.
5   https://www.washingtonpost.com/news/volokh-conspiracy/wp/ 2017/01/30/acting-attorney-general-orders-justice-department-attorneys-not-to-defend-immigration-executive-order/.
6   Ibid.
7   https://www.washingtonpost.com/news/volokh-conspiracy/wp/ 2017/01/30/acting-attorney-general-orders-justice-department-attorneys-not-to-defend-immigration-executive-order/.
8   The Supreme Court ultimately ruled that the executive proclamation that stemmed from that executive order was constitutional. This Supreme Court decision further confirmed just how mutinous her actions were.
9   http://www.judicialwatch.org/wp-content/uploads/2017/12/JW-v-DOJ-Yates-docs-Oct-17-00832-pg-4.pdf.
10 https://www.nytimes.com/2018/09/05/opinion/trump-white-house-anonymous-resistance.html.
11 https://www.thenewamerican.com/tech/environment/item/ 25324-retired-noaa-scientist-disputes-agency-s-study-denying-global-warming-hiatus?src=ilaw.
12 https://www.washingtonpost.com/news/the-fix/wp/2014/05/21/a-guide-to-the-va-and-the-scandals-engulfing-it/.

5. CRASHING THE TEA PARTY

1   *McCulloch v. Maryland*, 17 U.S. 316, 431 (1819), https://supreme
.justia.com/cases/federal/us/17/316/case.html.

2   http://www.washingtonexaminer.com/congressman-irs-asked-pro
life-group-about-the-content-of-their-prayers/article/2529924.

3   https://electionlawblog.org/?p=50160 (emphasis added).

4   https://thehill.com/policy/finance/197224-obama-not-a-smidgen-
of-corruption-behind-irs-targeting.

5   Ibid.

6   Jordan Sekulow and Matthew Clark, "SEKULOW & CLARK:
The IRS targeting scandal's smoking gun," *Washington Times*,
May 28, 2014, https://www.washingtontimes.com/news/2014/may/
28/sekulow-clark-the-irs-targeting-scandals-smoking-g/.

7   http://freebeacon.com/issues/judicial-watch-lois-lerner-doj-officials
and-fbi-met-to-plan-criminal-charges-for-obama-opponents/.

8   https://www.judicialwatch.org/press-room/press-releases/judicial-
watch-new-documents-reveal-doj-irs-and-fbi-plan-to-seek-
criminal-charges-of-obama-opponents/.

9   http://www.judicialwatch.org/document-archive/jw1559-00105/
(emphasis added).

10   https://www.washingtontimes.com/news/2017/oct/26/tea-party-
groups-targeted-irs-get-35-million-settl/.

11   https://www.washingtonpost.com/investigations/fallout-from-alle
gations-of-tea-party-targeting-hamper-irs-oversight-of-nonprofits/
2017/12/17/6403c1c0-c59e-11e7-a441-3a768c8586f1_story.html.

6. THE DEEP STATE SWAMP FESTERS AS THE VIRUS OF DECEPTION SPREADS

1   David Samuels, "The Aspiring Novelist Who Became Obama's
Foreign-Policy Guru," *New York Times*, May 5, 2016, http://www.ny
times.com/2016/05/08/magazine/the-aspiring-novelist-who-became-
obamas-foreign-policy-guru.html.

2   Brett T., "Gone in a Flash: James Rosen Reports His Iran Deal Question was Excised from Archives," Twitchy.com, May 9, 2016, 9:08 p.m., http://twitchy.com/brettt-3136/2016/05/09/gone-in-a-flash-james-rosen-reports-his-iran-deal-question-was-excised-from-archives-video/.

3   David Samuels, "The Aspiring Novelist Who Became Obama's Foreign-Policy Guru," *New York Times*, May 5, 2016, http://www.nytimes.com/2016/05/08/magazine/the-aspiring-novelist-who-became-obamas-foreign-policy-guru.html.

4   U.S. Department of State, Daily Press Briefing, December 2, 2013, https://2009-2017.state.gov/r/pa/prs/dpb/2013/12/218178.htm.

5   Ibid (emphasis added).

6   Ibid.

7   Ibid.

8   Ibid.

9   The entire Obama administration–era State Department website has since been archived, as is the normal procedure after a new administration takes office, so the video is naturally no longer on the current version of the State Department's website. We filed our FOIA request, however, while it was still on the site.

10   U.S. Department of State, Daily Press Briefing, December 2, 2013, http://video.state.gov/en/video/2886914568001 (last viewed May 10, 2016, 2:44 p.m.).

11   U.S. Department of State, Daily Press Briefing, December 2, 2013, YouTube, https://www.youtube.com/watch?v=zMSVRmM7_DM (last viewed May 10, 2016, 2:44 p.m.).

12   U.S. Department of State, Daily Press Briefing, May 10, 2016, https://2009-2017.state.gov/r/pa/prs/dpb/2016/05/257074.htm (last visited May 3, 2019).

13   https://www.reuters.com/article/us-usa-statedepartment-video/archived-state-department-briefing-video-deliberately-cut-idUS KCN0YN5R3.

14   http://www.washingtonexaminer.com/state-dept.-admits-altering video-of-2013-iran-press-conference/article/2592732.

15   http://media.aclj.org/pdf/Sensitive-State-Department-Memo-on-Iran-Video-Deletion.pdf.

16   Ibid.

17   Ibid.

18   http://www.washingtonexaminer.com/state-dept.-admits-altering
      video-of-2013-iran-press-conference/article/2592732.

19   John Solomon & Alison Spann, "FBI Uncovered Russian
      Bribery Plot Before Obama Administration Approved Controver-
      sial Nuclear Deal with Moscow," The Hill, October 17, 2017, 6:00
      a.m.,   http://thehill.com/policy/national-security/355749-fbi-
      uncovered-russian-bribery-plot-before-obama-administration.

20   Greg Price, "Did Russia Send Money to Bill Clinton's Foundation
      Like Trump Says? Fact-Checking the President's Claim," Newsweek,
      October 19, 2017, 11:19 a.m., http://www.newsweek.com/fact-
      check-clintons-russia-trump-688592.

21   Andrew C. McCarthy, "The Obama Administration's Uranium
      One Scandal," National Review, October 21, 2017, 4:00 a.m.,
      http://www.nationalreview.com/article/452972/uranium-one-deal-
      obama-administration-doj-hillary-clinton-racketeering.

22   http://thehill.com/policy/national-security/355749-fbi-uncovered-
      russian-bribery-plot-before-obama-administration.

23   Ibid.

24   https://www.nytimes.com/2015/04/24/us/cash-flowed-to-clinton-foun
      dation-as-russians-pressed-for-control-of-uranium-company.html.

25   Ibid.

26   http://www.newsweek.com/fact-check-clintons-russia-trump-6
      88592.

27   https://www.nationalreview.com/2017/10/uranium-one-deal-
      obama-administration-doj-hillary-clinton-racketeering/.

28   Ibid.

29   https://www.justice.gov/opa/pr/former-russian-nuclear-energy-of
      ficial-sentenced-48-months-prison-money-laundering-conspiracy.

30   http://www.foxnews.com/politics/2018/02/08/informant-says-
      moscow-paid-millions-in-bid-to-influence-clinton.html.

31   Ibid.

32   Eli Watkins, "Bill Clinton Meeting Causes Headaches for
      Hillary," CNN.com, June 20, 2016, 9:26 p.m., http://www.cnn
      .com/2016/06/29/politics/bill-clinton-loretta-lynch/.

NOTES

33   Alex Griswold, "Loretta Lynch Privately Meets with Bill Clinton Aboard Personal Plane," Mediaite.com, June 29, 2016, 1:22 p.m., http://www.mediaite.com/tv/loretta-lynch-privately-meetswith-bill-clinton-aboard-personal-plane/.

34   "Attorney General Lynch has Private Meeting with Bill Clinton," FoxNews.com, June 29, 2016, http://www.foxnews.com/politics/2016/06/29/attorney-general-lynch-meets-with-bill-clinton-priv ately.html.

35   Jesse Byrnes, "Lynch Meeting with Bill Clinton Creates Firestorm for Email Case," *The Hill*, June 30, 2016, 1:56 p.m., http://the hill.com/policy/national-security/286143-lynch-clinton-meeting-cr eates-firestorm.

36   Eli Watkins, "Bill Clinton Meeting Causes Headaches for Hillary," CNN.com, June 20, 2016, 9:26 p.m., http://www.cnn.com/2016/06/29/politics/bill-clinton-loretta-lynch/.

37   Josh Gerstein, "Judge Links Clinton Aide's Immunity to 'Criminal Investigation,'" Politico.com, June 14, 2016, 11:46 a.m., http://www.politico.com/story/2016/06/hillary-clinton-judge-inv estigation-224314; Stephen Dinan, "Judge Confirms 'Criminal Investigation' into Clinton Emails," WashingtonTimes.com, June 14, 2016, http://www.washingtontimes.com/news/2016/jun/14/judge-confirms-criminal-probe-clinton-emails/.

38   "White House Confirms 'Criminal' Probe over Clinton Emails, 'Shreds' Campaign Claim," FoxNews.com, Jun. 10, 2016, http://www.foxnews.com/politics/2016/06/10/white-house-confirms-criminal-probe-over-clinton-emails-shreds-campaign-claim.html.

39   "DOJ Acknowledges Hillary Email Investigation Is a 'Law Enforcement Matter,'" Insider.FoxNews.com, May 2, 2016, http://insider.foxnews.com/2016/05/02/judge-napolitano-new-dev elopments-hillary-clinton-email-investigation-justice-department.

40   https://thehill.com/policy/national-security/286849-fbi-didnt-rec ord-clinton-interview-no-sworn-oath.

41   https://www.wsj.com/articles/a-timeline-of-events-that-provided-original-basis-of-mueller-investigation-11553550282.

7. EXPOSING THE DEN OF VIPERS—THE ACLJ FOIA PRACTICE

1   https://www.foia.gov/faq.html.

2   *President Barack Obama, Memorandum for the Heads of Executive Departments and Agencies Re: Freedom of Information Act,* January 21, 2009, https://obamawhitehouse.archives.gov/the-press-office/freedom-information-act.

3   https://www.washingtonpost.com/blogs/erik-wemple/wp/2015/03/18/ap-obama-administration-sets-new-record-for-denying-records/; https://www.pbs.org/newshour/nation/obama-administration-sets-new-record-withholding-foia-requests; http://dailycaller.com/2016/03/18/new-data-shows-obama-least-transparent-prez-ever/; https://www.forbes.com/sites/realspin/2016/03/02/so-much-for-obamas-pledge-to-transparency/.

4   BleachBit is software that can be used to permanently delete computer files and emails. It was reported that Hillary Clinton's team used BleachBit making some of her emails impossible to recover. https://money.cnn.com/2016/08/26/technology/hillary-clinton-bleachbit/.

5   https://www.judicialwatch.org/press-room/press-releases/judicial-watch-new-documents-show-top-clinton-aide-alerted-email-inquiry/.

6   https://www.cnn.com/2018/05/04/politics/fbi-officials-lisa-page-james-baker-resign/index.html.

7   Ibid.

8   https://www.foxnews.com/politics/former-top-fbi-lawyer-james-baker-is-subject-of-federal-media-leak-probe-transcript-reveals.

9   Ibid.

10 Ibid.

11 Ibid.

12 Office of the Inspector General, U.S. Department of Justice, Oversight and Review Division 18-04, *A Review of Various Actions by the Federal Bureau of Investigation and Department of Justice in Advance of the 2016 Election,* June 2018 ("OIG Report"), https://www.justice.gov/file/1071991/download (last visited January 18, 2019).

13 Ibid, p. 48.

14   Ibid, p. 419. "FBI Attorney 1 reported to Deputy General Counsel Trisha Anderson, who in turn reported to then General Counsel James Baker." Ibid, p. 44.

15   Ibid, p. 419.

16   https://dailycaller.com/2018/10/04/fbi-dnc-lawyer-russia-2016election/.

17   Partially redacted copy of Comey's actual email made available by FBI on its "Vault" public website.

18   https://www.realclearpolitics.com/video/2018/03/18/turley_comey_may_have_lied_to_congress_under_oath_leaking_mccabe_firing_hurts_case.html.

19   https://heavy.com/news/2017/06/james-baker-fbi-general-counsel-bio-comey-trump-flynn-investigation/.

20   Ibid.

21   Ibid.

22   https://www.foxnews.com/politics/top-fbi-lawyer-baker-offers-explosive-testimony-on-abnormal-handling-of-russia-probe-into-trump-campaign-lawmakers.

23   https://www.washingtonexaminer.com/news/devin-nunes-says-ex-topfbi-lawyers-testimony-is-absolute-proof-of-fisa-abuse.

24   Ibid.

25   https://www.washingtonexaminer.com/news/top-fbi-lawyers-explosive-deposition-was-cut-short-jim-jordan-says.

26   See generally "Third Release" on file with author.

27   https://nypost.com/2018/06/27/sally-moyer-not-agent-5-in-igreport-on-fbi/ ("Clinesmith is 'FBI Attorney 2' in the report, while Moyer is, in fact, 'FBI Attorney 1,' which is not listed as one of the agents or lawyers cited for bias or referred for investigation.").

28   https://aclj.org/government-corruption/its-time-for-a-real-investigation-into-fired-fbi-director-james-comey.

29   https://aclj.org/government-corruption/crimes-corruption-and-congressional-deceptions-a-comey-of-errors.

30   On file with author, FBI 422.

31   On file with author, FBI 403, 406.

32   On file with author, FBI 468.

8. YOUR VOICE—GLOBAL IMPACT

1 https://www.theguardian.com/tv-and-radio/2018/oct/22/bring-back-our-girls-documentary-stolen-daughters-kidnapped-boko-haram.
2 Hebrews 13:3, Holy Bible (NASB).
3 https://aclj.org/persecuted-church/62-page-indictment-against-american-pastor-andrew-brunson-effectively-calls-sharing-the-gospel-an-act-of-terrorism.
4 Luke 18:1–8, Holy Bible (NIV).
5 https://www.congress.gov/104/plaws/publ45/PLAW-104publ45.pdf.
6 https://www.whitehouse.gov/presidential-actions/presidential-proclamation-recognizing-jerusalem-capital-state-israel-relocating-united-states-embassy-israel-jerusalem/.

9. DEFEATING GENOCIDE

1 U.S.C. § 1091 (2012).
2 Convention on the Prevention and Punishment of the Crime of Genocide, art. II, Dec. 9, 1948.
3 "Genocide Against Christians in the Middle East," Knights of Columbus and in Defense of Christians, March 9, 2016, http://indefenseofchristians.org/wp-content/uploads/2016/03/Genocide-report.pdf.
4 Bureau of Democracy, H.R. and Lab., U.S. Department of State, *Syria 2014 International Religious Freedom Report* (*"Syria Report"*) 2 (2014).
5 Bureau of Democracy, H.R. and Lab., U.S. Department of State, *Iraq 2014 International Religious Freedom Report* (*"Iraq Report"*) 3 (2014).
6 "Genocide Against Christians in the Middle East," Knights of Columbus and in Defense of Christians, March 9, 2016, http://indefenseofchristians.org/wp-content/uploads/2016/03/Genocide-report.pdf; *see also Syria Report.*

7   *Syria Report*, p. 1.

8   Katie Mansfield, "Barbaric ISIS Mangle 250 Children in Industrial Dough Kneader and Cooks Rest Alive in Oven," Express.co.UK.com, October 26, 2016, 4:00 p.m., http://www.express.co.uk/news/world/723942/ISIS-kills-250-children-dough-kneader-burns-men-alive-oven-Syria-Open-Doors-report.

9   Ibid.

10 *Syria Report*, p. 11.

11 *Iraq Report*, p. 2.

12 http://media.aclj.org/pdf/LTR-Umarov-1-1-18_Redacted.pdf.

13 http://media.aclj.org/pdf/LTR-Umarov-1-1-18_Redacted.pdf (internal citations omitted).

14 Ibid (internal citations omitted).

15 Ibid (internal citations omitted).

16 Ibid (internal citations omitted).

17 Elise Labott and Tal Kopan, "John Kerry: *ISIS Responsible for Genocide*," CNN.com, March 18, 2016, updated 2:41 p.m., http://www.cnn.com/2016/03/17/politics/us-iraq-syria-genocide/index.html.

18 Erin Dooley and Kirit Radia, "'ISIS is Clearly Responsible for Genocide,' Tillerson Says," ABCNews.go.com, August 15, 2017, http://abcnews.go.com/International/isis-responsible-genocide-tillerson/story?id=49231365.

19 https://aclj.org/persecuted-church/aclj-launches-seven-point-plan in-campaign-to-stop-isis-genocide-against-christians.

20 Ibid (internal citations omitted).

21 S.C. Res. 2379, ¶ 2 (September 21, 2017), https://undocs.org/S/RES/2379(2017).

22 http://media.aclj.org/pdf/Signed-letter-to-H.E.-Ban-Ki-moon-04.28.2016_Redacted.pdf.

23 http://reliefweb.int/sites/reliefweb.int/files/resources/160506SRSGUNSCBriefing-ASPREPARED.doc.pdf.

24 http://media.aclj.org/pdf/Letter-UNHRC-States-Members_Redacted.pdf.

25 http://media.aclj.org/pdf/LTR-AdamaDieng-8-22-2016_Redacted.pdf.

26   http://media.aclj.org/pdf/Bessho-LTR-11-28-16_Redacted.pdf
      (emphasis added).
27   http://media.aclj.org/pdf/LTR-FareedYasseen-(Iraqi-Amb.-to-
      US)-12-19-16_Redacted-(FINAL-1)(1).pdf.
28   http://media.aclj.org/pdf/LTR-AntonioGuterres_Redacted.pdf.
29   http://media.aclj.org/pdf/LTR-
      AdamaDieng-7-10-17_Redacted.pdf.
30   http://media.aclj.org/pdf/LTR-France-7-24-17_Redacted.pdf.
31   http://media.aclj.org/pdf/10DowningStreet-responseltr.pdf.
32   http://media.aclj.org/pdf/LTR-UKgovernment_Redacted.pdf.
33   Ibid.
34   http://media.aclj.org/pdf/LetterFromUN-Re-Genocide-912-17.pdf
      (emphasis added).
35   Ibid (emphasis added).
36   https://undocs.org/S/2017/710.
37   http://www.un.org/en/ga/search/view_doc.asp?symbol=S/RES/
      2379(2017).
38   http://media.aclj.org/pdf/LTR-Guterres-10-16-17_Redacted.pdf.
39   http://media.aclj.org/pdf/LTR-
      AdamaDieng-9-29-17_Redacted.pdf.
40   https://aclj.org/persecuted-church/isis-brutality-against-chris
      tians-inthe-philippines-has-been-unthinkable (emphasis added).
41   https://aclj.org/persecuted-church/delivering-aid-to-christians-
      facing-genocide-in-iraq.
42   http://media.aclj.org/pdf/LTR-UKgovernment_Redacted.pdf
      (emphasis added).
43   https://aclj.org/persecuted-church/defending-christians-facing-
      genocide-at-the-un-human-rights-council.
44   http://thehill.com/homenews/administration/357224-pence-says-
      us-to-stop-funding-ineffective-un-relief-efforts.
45   https://www.usaid.gov/news-information/press-releases/jul
      6-2017-us-government-provides-150-million-iraq-stabilization.
46   http://www.foxnews.com/politics/2018/01/11/pence-promise-ful
      filled-us-changes-rules-on-un-to-help-christian-and-minority-
      victims-genocide-in-iraq.html.
47   https://www.usaid.gov/news-information/press-releases/jan8-20

18-continued-us-assistance-to-better-meet-the-needs-of-min
orities-in-iraq.

48   Ibid.

49   http://www.foxnews.com/politics/2018/01/11/pence-promise-ful
filled-us-changes-rules-on-un-to-help-christian-and-minority-vic
tims-genocide-in-iraq.html.

50   http://www.foxnews.com/politics/2018/01/11/pence-promise-ful
filled-us-changes-rules-on-un-to-help-christian-and-minority-
victims-genocide-in-iraq.html.

51   http://media.aclj.org/pdf/letter-from-the-RT-HON-ALISTAIR-B
URT-MP_Redacted.pdf.

52   https://aclj.org/persecuted-church/uk-responds-to-aclj-on-gen
ocide-working-to-ensure-christians-can-return-to-their-homes-
and-flourish.

10. FIGHTING FOR LIFE AND WINNING: DEFEATING THE ABORTION DISTORTION

1   https://www.liveaction.org/news/these-are-the-4-m
ost-prevalent-abortion-procedures-in-america/.

2   https://aclj.org/pro-life/new-york-governor-signs-unfathomable-
law-that-allows-abortions-all-the-way-up-to-birth.

3   https://votesmart.org/public-statement/970210/issue-position-p
rotecting-innocent-life#.XE1Tf6eZMXp.

4   https://www.cbsnews.com/news/andrew-cuomo-hillary-clinton-ab
ortion-rights-new-york-roe-v-wade-womens-rights/.

5   https://www.cbsnews.com/news/andrew-cuomo-hillary-clinton-a
bortion-rights-new-york-roe-v-wade-womens-rights/.

6   https://www.nytimes.com/2019/01/07/nyregion/cuomo-abortion-
roe-vs-wade.html.

7   https://www.amny.com/news/clinton-cuomo-abortion-rights-1.2
5657795.

8   https://www.washingtontimes.com/news/2019/jan/23/one-world-
trade-center-lit-pink-celebration-new-yo/.

9   https://www.humancoalition.org/graphics/3000-babies-aborted-every-day/.

10   https://twitter.com/PPact/status/1087871219913932800.

11   https://www.nyclu.org/en/news/huge-wins-reproductive-justice-voting-rights-and-trans-new-yorkers (emphasis added).

12   https://www.lifenews.com/2019/01/24/vermont-bill-would-legalize-abortion-up-to-birth-unborn-baby-shall-not-have-independent-rights-under-law/.

13   As reported by LifeNews.com:

> The *Providence Journal* reports there are two competing pro-abortion bills in the Rhode Island House. State Rep. Edith Ajello's bill is the more radically pro-abortion of the two. It also is the one that Planned Parenthood and the American Civil Liberties Union support.
>
> Both bills appear to allow restrictions for late-term abortions, but they add a broad "health" exception for abortions after viability. The exception would allow women to abort unborn babies up to nine months of pregnancy for basically any "health" reason, including "age, economic, social and emotional factors," a definition given by the U.S. Supreme Court in the case *Doe v. Bolton*. Ajello's bill also would allow partial-birth abortions.

https://www.lifenews.com/2019/01/24/rhode-island-bill-would-follow-new-yorks-and-legalize-abortions-up-to-birth/.

14   https://www.nationalreview.com/corner/virginia-bill-would-legalize-abortion-up-to-birth/.

15   https://www.npr.org/2016/10/19/498293478/fact-check-trump-and-clinton-s-final-presidential-debate.

16   https://www.desiringgod.org/articles/we-know-they-are-killing-children-all-of-us-know.

17   https://aclj.org/abortion/pro-abortion-mob-shouts-hail-satan-battle-life-battle-good-evil.

18   http://www.washingtonpost.com/blogs/on-faith/wp/2013/05/09/kermit-gosnell-and-the-abortion-movement-in-defense-of-the-defenseless/.

19   https://www.washingtontimes.com/news/2018/oct/8/some-kavanaugh-protesters-were-paid-journalist/.

20 https://www.usatoday.com/story/news/2019/01/18/march-life-r
ally-thousands-washington-say-all-life-matters/2613673002/.

21 https://www.washingtontimes.com/news/2019/jan/18/march-life-k
icks-students-stream-nations-capital-p/.

22 https://www.cnn.com/2019/01/18/politics/march-for-life/index.html.

23 https://www.hhs.gov/about/news/2019/01/18/hhs-is-committed-t
o-protecting-life-and-conscience.html.

24 https://www.hhs.gov/about/news/2019/01/18/trump-
administration-actions-to-protect-life-and-conscience.html.

25 https://www.politico.com/story/2017/12/08/justice-department-plan
ned-parenthood-fetal-tissue-transfers-215999; https://www.grassley.s
enate.gov/news/news-releases/grassley-refers-planned-parenthood-fe
tal-tissue-procurement-organizations-fbi; https://www1.cbn.com/
cbnnews/us/2018/january/planned-parenthoods-cecile-richards-
stepping-down-leaving-atrail-of-misery-in-her-wake.

26 https://www1.cbn.com/cbnnews/us/2018/january/planned-parenthood
s-cecile-richards-stepping-down-leaving-a-trail-of-misery-in-her-wake.

27 https://www.prochoiceamerica.org/2017/11/13/naral-supreme-
court-challenge-reproductive-health-law/.

28 https://oag.ca.gov/news/press-releases/attorney-general-kamala-
d-harris-13-other-attorneys-general-file-amicus-brief.

29 https://aclj.org/pro-life/aclj-defends-pro-life-speech-and-pro-life-
pregnancy-centers-from-being-forced-to-promote-abortion-at-
supreme-court.

30 https://www.prochoiceamerica.org/2017/11/13/naral-supreme-
court-challenge-reproductive-health-law/.

31 In conjunction with its landmark decision in *National Institute of
Family and Life Advocates v. Becerra*, 585 U.S. _____ (2018), the
Supreme Court issued a GVR in our case (an order granting our
petition for certiorari, vacating the decision of the Ninth Circuit
Court of Appeals, and remanding to the lower court for reconsid-
eration in light of its opinion).

32 https://aclj.org/pro-life/pro-life-pregnancy-centers-vindicated-in-
california.

33 https://aclj.org/pro-life/hhs-to-california-targeting-pro-life-p
regnancy-centers-violates-federal-law.

NOTES

34   *Gee v. Planned Parenthood of Gulf Coast, Inc.*, 586 U.S. ____ (2018) (Thomas, J., dissenting) (internal citation omitted), https://www.supremecourt.gov/orders/courtorders/121018zor_f2ah.pdf.

35   https://www.politifact.com/oregon/statements/2013/jan/26/gayle atteberry/are-abortion-clinics-oregon-not-held-basic-health-/.

36   https://savethestorks.com/2018/01/birds-legal-rights-unborn-chi ldren-america/.

37   https://aclj.org/pro-life/supreme-court-pro-life-pregnancy-centers-cant-be-forced-to-promote-abortion.

38   https://aclj.org/pro-life/two-briefs-filed-in-fight-to-expose-illegal-abortion-practices.

39   https://www.npr.org/2019/01/02/681208228/trumps-judicial-ap pointments-were-confirmed-at-historic-pace-in-2018; https://thehill.com/homenews/senate/385728-republicans-confirming-trumps-court-nominees-at-record-pace.

11. FAKE NEWS

1   https://www.snopes.com/fact-check/sarah-palin-russia-house/.

2   http://www.nbcnews.com/id/6055248/ns/politics/t/cbs-news-ad mits-bush-documents-cant-be-verified/#.XNCEq6Z7mCc.

3   https://www.buzzfeednews.com/article/jasonleopold/trump-russia-cohen-moscow-tower-mueller-investigation.

4   https://www.cnbc.com/2019/01/18/trump-directed-cohen-to-lie-to-congress-about-moscow-project-report.html.

5   https://www.axios.com/trump-told-cohen-lie-congress-moscow-tower-fb2b1c98-9773-41c7-b350-56bcc30be972.html.

6   https://www.cnn.com/2019/01/17/politics/buzzfeed-trump-cohen-lie-congress-moscow/index.html.

7   Ibid.

8   https://www.foxnews.com/politics/mueller-team-disputes-buzzfeed-report-claiming-trump-told-cohen-to-lie.

9   https://twitter.com/realDonaldTrump/status/108645 8937002680320.

10   http://www.washingtonpost.com/blogs/fact-checker/wp/2015/08/

12/for-planned-parenthood-abortion-stats-3-percent-and-94-p
ercent-are-both-misleading/.

11 http://issuu.com/actionfund/docs/ppfa_financials_
2010_122711_web_vf?e=1994783/2039600.

12 https://www.plannedparenthood.org/uploads/filer_public/80/d7/
80d7d7c7-977c-4036-9c61-b3801741b441/190118-annualre-
port18-p01.pdf.

13 https://www.plannedparenthood.org/uploads/filer_public/80/d7/
80d7d7c7-977c-4036-9c61-b3801741b441/190118-annualre-
port18-p01.pdf.

14 https://www.plannedparenthood.org/uploads/filer_public/80/d7/
80d7d7c7-977c-4036-9c61-b3801741b441/190118-annualrepo
rt18-p01.pdf.

15 https://aclj.org/media-abortion-distortion-plays-abortion-in
dustry-deception.

16 http://issuu.com/actionfund/docs/ppfa_financials_2010_12
2711_web_vf?mode=window&viewMode=doublePage.

17 http://www.plannedparenthood.org/files/PPFA/fact_ppser
vices_2011-01-13.pdf.

18 https://www.plannedparenthood.org/uploads/filer_public/80/d7/
80d7d7c7-977c-4036-9c61-b3801741b441/190118-annualrepor-
t18-p01.pdf.

19 https://aclj.org/media-abortion-distortion-plays-abortion-ind
ustry-deception.

20 https://www.lifenews.com/2012/09/05/media-hides-fact-planned-p
arenthood-does-40-of-abortions/.

21 http://mediamatters.org/research/2011/02/18/laura-ingraham-g
rossly-misrepresents-planned-pa/176611.

22 https://www.washingtonpost.com/news/fact-checker/wp/2015/08/
12/for-planned-parenthood-abortion-stats-3-percent-and-94-p
ercent-are-both-misleading/.

23 https://aclj.org/pro-life/wapo-three-pinocchios-for-planned-par
enthoods-3-percent-abortion-lie.

24 http://www.lifenews.com/2012/09/05/media-hides-fact-planned-p
arenthood-does-40-of-abortions/.

25 http://www.washingtonpost.com/blogs/fact-checker/wp/2015/08/

12/for-planned-parenthood-abortion-stats-3-percent-and-94-p
ercent-are-both-misleading/.

26 http://www.lifenews.com/2012/09/05/media-hides-fact-planned-p
arenthood-does-40-of-abortions/.

27 http://www.washingtonpost.com/blogs/fact-checker/wp/2015/08/
12/for-planned-parenthood-abortion-stats-3-percent-and-94-p
ercent-are-both-misleading/.

28 Ibid.

29 http://www.lifenews.com/2012/09/05/media-hides-fact-planned-p
arenthood-does-40-of-abortions/.

30 http://www.washingtonpost.com/blogs/fact-checker/about-the-f
act-checker/.

31 https://aclj.org/pro-life/wapo-three-pinocchios-for-planned-
parenthoods-3-percent-abortion-lie.

32 http://www.washingtonpost.com/blogs/fact-checker/wp/2015/08/12/
for-planned-parenthood-abortion-stats-3-percent-and-94-percent-a
re-both-misleading/.

33 Ibid.

34 https://www.washingtonpost.com/national/health-science/planne
d-parenthood-taps-baltimore-health-commissioner-as-president/
2018/09/12/63483256-b6b7-11e8-a2c5-3187f427e253_story.html.

35 https://aclj.org/radio-tv/schedule.

36 U.S. Const. amend. I.

12. THE SACRED DUTY TO VOTE

1 https://www.politico.com/mapdata-2016/2016-election/results/
map/president/.

2 https://www.usatoday.com/story/news/2017/12/21/virginia-
election-tie-coin-tosses-picking-names-hat-yep-thats-how-races-
decided-probably-never-going/973630001/.

3 https://www.cbsnews.com/news/virginia-abortion-bill-proposed-by-
kathy-tran-third-trimester-today-2019-01-30/.

4 https://www.elections.virginia.gov/Files/Registration-Statistics/
2017/01/Registrant_Count_By_House.pdf.

5   Romans 13:1, Holy Bible (ESV).

6   Romans 13:4, Holy Bible (NASB).

7   Romans 13:6–7, Holy Bible (NASB).

8   Matthew 25:14–30, Holy Bible (NASB).

9   Proverbs 29:2, Holy Bible (ESV).

10   Deuteronomy 1:13, Holy Bible (ESV).

11   1 Timothy 2:1–2, Holy Bible (ESV).

12   Philippians 3:20, Holy Bible (ESV).

13   Mark 12:17, Holy Bible (NIV).

14   John 17:14–15, Holy Bible.

15   Romans 13:1, Holy Bible (NLT).

16   Psalm 146:3, Holy Bible (ESV).

17   See 1 Samuel 13:14, Holy Bible.

18   What 2 Thessalonians 3:10 actually says is, "For even when we were with you, we used to give you this order: if anyone is not willing to work, then he is not to eat, either." 2 Thessalonians 3:10, Holy Bible (NASB).

19   https://aclj.org/free-speech-2/county-backtracks-decides-not-to-violate-right-of-assembly-with-proposal-that-could-cripple-home-bible-studies.

20   https://aclj.org/free-speech/virginia-county-to-interrogate-homeschool-teens-about-their-religious-beliefs.

21   https://aclj.org/religious-liberty/aclj-challenges-buddhist-meditation-practices-in-public-schools.

22   http://www.washingtonexaminer.com/virginia-county-takes-aim-at-home-bible-studies-freedom-of-assembly/article/2548301.

23   https://aclj.org/free-speech-2/county-backtracks-decides-not-to-violate-right-of-assembly-with-proposal-that-could-cripple-home-bible-studies.

24   https://aclj.org/free-speech/virginia-county-to-interrogate-homeschool-teens-about-their-religious-beliefs.

25   https://www.wsj.com/articles/help-is-on-the-way-for-middle-eastern-christians-1528931329.

26   https://aclj.org/persecuted-church/genocide-the-problem-from-hell-continues.

27 https://aclj.org/persecuted-church/isis-expands-jihadist-genocide-bombs-egyptian-christians-on-palm-sunday.

28 https://www.bbc.com/news/world-asia-48059328.

29 https://aclj.org/persecuted-church/isis-brutality-against-christians-in-the-philippines-has-been-unthinkable.

30 Romans 13:4, Holy Bible (NASB).

31 https://2009-2017.state.gov/secretary/remarks/2016/03/254782.htm.

32 http://www.foxnews.com/politics/2017/12/07/planned-parenthood-under-investigation-by-justice-department-over-sale-fetal-tissue.html.

13. REDRESS OF GRIEVANCES

1 https://obamawhitehouse.archives.gov/the-press-office/2010/08/09/remarks-president-a-dnc-finance-event-austin-texas.

2 U.S. Const. amend. I.

3 Ibid (emphasis added).

4 Ibid.

5 https://aclj.org/free-speech-2/end-irs-abuse.

6 U.S. Const. amend. I.

7 https://www.washingtontimes.com/news/2017/oct/26/tea-party-groups-targeted-irs-get-35-million-settl/.

INDEX

Abedin, Huma, 96–97
abortion, 154–177
   Hillary Clinton on late-term,
     158–159
   and Hyde Amendment, 155,
     164
   and importance of local elec-
     tions, 16
   and Mexico City Policy, 31,
     155, 168–169
   New York State's radical legal-
     ization of, 156–161, 170, 198
   partial-birth, 158–159
   and Planned Parenthood, 21,
     28, 157, 208, 213, 214, 221
   the radical Left and, 154–158,
     160–163, 221
   and Supreme Court, 161–163,
     173–175
   taxpayer funding for, 6, 155,
     213
   and "3 percent lie," 186–192
   Donald Trump on late-term,
     159
   and Virginia's Repeal Act, 158,
     198
   "abortion distortion," 172–177,
     186
ACLJ. *See* American Center for
   Law and Justice
ACLU (American Civil Liberties
   Union), 157
Acosta, Jim, 180
Affordable Care Act (ACA, Oba-
   macare), 2, 3, 13, 15, 19–21,
   28, 31, 53, 167–168, 186, 214
Aid to the Church in Need, 127
al-Baghdadi, Abu Bakr, 123
Al Qaa, Lebanon, 128, 129
Aleppo, Syria, 127–128
Alito, Samuel, 174
Amaq (Islamic State news
   agency), 129
American Center for Law and
   Justice (ACLJ), IX–XIII, 193,
   224
   and abortion issue, 16, 169,
     170, 173, 176, 186–187

and battle against Deep State, 69–70, 91

and Clinton-Lynch meeting, 87–90

defense of persecuted Christians by, 111–113, 123–125, 135–140, 212–213

FOIA requests/lawsuits filed by, 82–83, 92–109

limits to power of, 78–79

and Obama IRS, 27, 54–58, 60–62, 66

petition campaigns led by, 219–220

and political leadership, 153

purpose of, 24

and religious freedom, 207, 208

and relocation of U.S. Embassy to Jerusalem, 118

and Supreme Court, 173

American Civil Liberties Union (ACLU), 157

Anderson, Trisha, 102

Antifa, 25

APCO Worldwide, 83

Arizona, 190

ARMZ, 80

atheists, 206

Axios, 183

Azar, Alex, 165

Baker, James, 100–107, 109

ballot referenda, 5

Baltimore, Maryland, 16

Ban Ki-moon, 96, 139

Band, Doug, 96, 97

Barnard College, 157

Bart, Alistair, 148–149

"Be-on-the-Lookout" (BOLO) lists, 62

Bibi, Asia, 116–117

"big picture" approach, 28

bipartisanship, 14

BleachBit, 85

Boehner, John, 224

Boko Haram, 111

BOLO lists, 62

border wall, 14

Boston Tea Party, 49–50

Brandeis, Louis, 94

Brazile, Donna, 29

BringBackOurGirls, 111

Brunson, Andrew, 113–116

Buddhism, 208

buffer zones, free speech, 173

Bureau of Public Affairs (State Department), 77

Bush, George W., and administration, 41, 74, 119, 181–182, 197

BuzzFeed, 181–185

California, 16, 59–61, 166, 170–171

campaign promises, 14, 19–23, 30

Canada, 79, 81

candidates, political, X–XI, 12–15

Cantor, Eric, 224–225

Carson, Ben, 156

Carter administration, 39

CBS News, 156–157

Central Intelligence Agency (CIA), 41–42

CFIUS. See Committee on Foreign Investments in the United States

CFPB (Consumer Financial Protection Bureau), 46

child-safety seats, 16–17
"chilling" effect (of legislation),
    223
China, 199
Choi, Rob, 60
Christians and Christianity, 10,
    110–114, 116, 117, 122–143,
    145–153, 196, 197, 199,
    202–207, 211–213
CIA (Central Intelligence
    Agency), 41–42
Cincinnati, Ohio, 56, 58–61
citizenry, informed, 93
Clark, Matthew, XII–XIII,
    208–210
Clinesmith, Kevin, 105
Clinton, Bill, 80, 81, 84, 87, 89,
    96, 119
Clinton, Hillary Rodham, 29,
    79–87, 89, 90, 96–98, 100, 105,
    156–158, 185
Clinton Foundation, 24, 36, 63,
    76, 80–82, 96–98
"Clinton Machine," 185
CMS, 168
CNN, 84, 180, 183, 184
Coats-Snowe Amendment, 166
Cohen, Michael, 182–186
Comey, James, 42, 46, 85–91,
    100–107, 109, 185
Commission on International Re-
    ligious Freedom, 135
Committee on Foreign Invest-
    ments in the United States
    (CFIUS), 79–80, 82
Congress. See also House of Rep-
    resentatives; Senate
    2010 midterm elections, 26
    2012 elections, 53

2020 elections, 213–214
    and abortion, 155, 165, 214
    James Baker and, 102–103
    broken promises by, 30
    Michael Cohen and, 182–184
    James Comey and, 100, 103,
        106–107, 185
    demanding integrity from
        members of, 23
    and First Amendment, 219
    and Freedom of Information
        Act, 93
    grassroots actions directed at,
        194, 207–208, 220
    and Guantanamo closing, 98
    and importance of local poli-
        tics, 18, 226
    and Obama IRS scandal, 63,
        66–67
    and Obamacare, 20
    and persecution of Christians,
        137
    and Planned Parenthood, 21
    and relocation of U.S. Em-
        bassy in Israel, 118–121
    Republican control of, 2–4
    and Second Amendment, 221
    and Tea Party, 224
    unpopularity of, 22
    Sally Yates and, 44
Conscience and Freedom Divi-
    sion (of Office for Civil
    Rights), 167
conservatives
    and 2016 election, 35
    and 2020 election, 10
    and campaign promises, 14
    and control of the House, 2, 5,
        7

in the courts, 21, 31–32, 213
and Deep State, 1, 4, 36, 37, 42
engagement by, 24
failure of, to implement
    agenda, 28
and fake news, 178, 193–194
and free speech, 207
grassroots activism by, 26,
    49–54, 57–68, 222–224
and healthcare, 15
importance of voting by,
    196–197
need for political dominance
    by, 2
need for unity among, 226
and "old rules," 3
and red wave, 1
and Republican Party, 2, 29
targeting of, 27, 32, 227
in Tea Party, 217, 218, 223
and Donald Trump's agenda,
    18
and understanding the big pic-
    ture, 118
in Virginia, 158
Consumer Financial Protection
    Bureau (CFPB), 46
Convention on the Prevention
    and Punishment of the Crime
    of Genocide, 123, 130–132,
    147
Coptic Christians, 128
Cordray, Richard, 46
corruption. *See also specific scan-
    dals, e.g.:* Uranium One
    Christians and, 203
    and Deep State, 47, 48, 60, 68,
        69, 91
    of DNC, 29

at FBI, 63–65, 100–104, 106
FOIA and uncovering of, 92,
    96, 98–100
and human nature, 107–109
at IRS, 58, 59, 66–68, 216
and the "swamp," 58
county commissions, 9
Cuomo, Andrew, 156–157

DACA (Deferred Action for
    Childhood Arrivals), 14–15
Daily Caller, 102–103
Danbury Baptist Association, 205
Deep State, XI, XIII, 35–48
    ACLJ's battle with the, 69–70,
        92, 147
    and Clinton-Lynch meeting,
        84–91
    and "draining the swamp," 69
    and FOIA, 95–96, 98, 99
    and government corruption,
        107–109
    and government leaks, 40–42
    and intelligence apparatus, 42
    and Iran nuclear deal, 70–79
    IRS as weapon of, 49–53, 60,
        65, 68, 222
    reality of, 35–36
    red wave as threat to, 62, 227
    regulatory, 28
    Tea Party as enemy of,
        216–219, 222
    tenacity of, 33
    thwarting of America by, 37
    Donald Trump and, 3
    undermining of conservative
        agenda by, 1, 4
    and Uranium One deal, 80–84
    and Yates affair, 43–48